NOTES FROM CANADA'S YOUNG ACTIVISTS

compiled and edited by

Severn Cullis-Suzuki

Kris Frederickson

Ahmed Kayssi

Cynthia Mackenzie

with **Daniel Aldana Cohen**

NOTES FROM **CANADA'S**

YOUNG

ACTIVISTS

A GENERATION
STANDS UP FOR CHANGE

GREYSTONE BOOKS
Douglas & McIntyre Publishing Group
Vancouver/Toronto/Berkeley

07 08 09 10 11   5 4 3 2 1

Greystone Books
A division of Douglas & McIntyre Ltd.
2323 Quebec Street, Suite 201
Vancouver, British Columbia
Canada V5T 4S7
www.greystonebooks.com

Library and Archives Canada Cataloguing in Publication
Notes from Canada's young activists : a generation stands up for change /
compiled and edited by Severn Cullis-Suzuki... [et al.].
Includes bibliographical references.

ISBN 978-1-55365-237-3

1. Social action—Canada. 2. Young adults—Canada—Political activity.
I. Cullis-Suzuki, Severn
HN107.N68 2007   361.2'0971   C2006-906749-X

Editing by Nancy Flight and Iva Cheung
Cover design by Peter Cocking
Text design by Naomi MacDougall
Photo of Jessica Lax by Jocelyn Land-Murphy; of Severn Cullis-Suzuki
by David Strongman; of Miali-Elise Coley by Becky Kilabuk; of Chris
Richards courtesy of Marie Brown Photography; of Ben Peterson by
Catherine Farquharson; of Craig Kielburger courtesy of the Free The
Children Project; and of Kris Frederickson by Sara Williscroft.
Printed and bound in Canada by Friesens
Printed on acid-free paper that is forest friendly (100% post-consumer
recycled paper) and has been processed chlorine free.
Distributed in the U.S. by Publishers Group West

We gratefully acknowledge the financial support of the Canada Council
for the Arts, the British Columbia Arts Council, the Province of British
Columbia through the Book Publishing Tax Credit, and the Government
of Canada through the Book Publishing Industry Development Program
(BPIDP) for our publishing activities.

CONTENTS

ix *Foreword by Dr. Samantha Nutt*

1 *Introduction*

7 Art, Politics, and Questioning Authority
   Ilona Dougherty

13 A Reference Letter to Remember
   George Roter

21 Building a Nation of Nations:
   Aboriginal Youth and Canadian Politics
   Ginger Gosnell-Myers

28 It's About Time
   Anil Patel

35 Rooting for Change
   Severn Cullis-Suzuki

41 Swimming in the Fast Lane
   Karen Kun

49 Catching the Spirit
   D. Simon Jackson

58 Lessons from Making the Jump:
   A Young Person's Experience in Politics
   Lyndsay Poaps

67 The Sunday Suppers
   Richard Hoshino

74   Modern Inuk on the Move
      Miali-Elise Coley

81   Remembering the Dance: Feeling My Way to Freedom
      Annahid Dashtgard

90   Departure
      Ahmed Kayssi

96   Free The Children: The World's Largest Network of
      Children Helping Children through Education
      Craig Kielburger

106   Reasons to Dream
      Jessica Lax

115   Finding Home:
      Storytelling, South Asians, and Spirituality
      Shakil Choudhury

125   "Ah. So We Are All the Same": Reflections on Human
      Development and Attitudes in Activism
      Chris Richards

137   dub poetics and personal politics
      d'bi.young.anitafrika

149   On Authority and Activism
      Robin Rix

156   Watershed Moments of a Métis Mentor
      Kris Frederickson

164   In, and Out Again
      Cynthia Mackenzie

171 Emergence from Colonialism:
     Memories and Stories of Bantu Life
     Devi Mucina

182 Writing the Wrong
     Ben Peterson

189 Finding the "I" in Action:
     Defining Activism to Include Me
     Natalie Gerum

197 Gardom Lake to Tatamagouche: Climate Change,
     the WTO, and a Community Land Trust
     Yuill Herbert

205 Challenging the Planet: A Call from the Arctic
     to Face the Heat on Climate Change
     Tim Harvey

215 *Further Reading*

223 *Acknowledgements*

225 *About the Editors*

Dr. Samantha Nutt

ARE ACTIVISTS BORN, or do they evolve out of life's inevitable twists and turns?

I was around fourteen years old when I realized that I was that reliably irritating person in the classroom who wouldn't take no for an answer—the one who could always be suckered by her peers into regaling the teacher with a never-ending chorus of "But it's not right!" and "That's not fair!" In what I can only assume was an attempt at retribution, an early English teacher of mine helped the class understand the idiom "having a bee in one's bonnet" by using me as the reference point. My uncompromising nature, in those early years, led to a lot of time spent in detention.

It's little wonder, then, that I ended up finding my life's work in war zones—the reality of the injustice, the suffering, and the degradation afflicting those living with war around the world *isn't* right, and it *isn't* fair. It was through witnessing, first hand, the horror of war (while I could still confidently check the "youth" demographic box) that I came to understand the importance of having a voice in something more meaningful than an onerous homework assignment and to discover the paradoxical sadness and joy that inevitably come with a "calling."

The following collection of stories—reflections from many of Canada's brightest young thinkers—is a testament to the potential that exists in each of us to make our voices heard and to make a difference on pressing social issues. Miali-Elise Coley reminds us that this country needs to learn from the Inuit and from their traditional way of life, which is rooted in a deep respect for the environment and for racial diversity. Ilona Dougherty, founder of Apathy is Boring, continues to develop new and creative ways to combat complacency and engage youth in politics. Ahmed Kayssi, whose family found their way to Canada from their home country of war-torn Iraq, teaches racial and religious tolerance—one person at a time. Severn Cullis-Suzuki offers a beautiful tribute to the balance and bounty that exist within nature and upon which humankind depends. These and the other stories featured in *Notes from Canada's Young Activists* give us a first-hand look at those who are prepared to put it all on the line for a cause and how they arrived at this decision so early in life. Collectively, they offer something rarely captured so effectively in print: genuine hope. At a time when war, violence, cultural assimilation, natural disasters, and climate change emerge as problems that appear so overwhelming that they become paralytic, it is liberating to read about those who are championing a new ethos. It is impossible for anyone reading this book to walk away lamenting that it's too difficult to know where to start or what to do. All of these young activists have websites. Send them an email, make a donation, join in their efforts. Don't wait!

Over my years as Executive Director of War Child Canada, I have met and spoken with many interesting people across Canada as part of our effort to inform public thinking about what it means to be a good global citizen. What has struck me is how much easier it is for most people to articulate what they are against rather than what they are for. This trait is, in many respects, part of the Canadian identity: we don't always know what we are,* but we know what we're not. The activists contributing to this book, by comparison, have made that leap— they know what they stand for, and they draw strength from an unrelenting belief in the positive role individuals and communities can play in effecting social change. Perhaps this self-assuredness, more than anything else, is what makes them extraordinary Canadians. This and the fact that they are also part of an elusive assortment of individuals who—for better or for worse—steadfastly refuse to give up at the first "no."

More than two decades ago, in response to one of my earliest rants about something mundane in the middle of a computer science lab, the teacher (visibly irritated) shouted, "This

---

*For example, Canadians (including youth) have very sentimental views of our contribution to peacekeeping efforts around the world. A War Child Canada national youth opinion poll carried out in partnership with the polling firm Environics in 2005 found that young Canadians ranked peacekeeping as Canada's most positive contribution to the world, followed by foreign aid (the results are accurate within a margin of error of 4.3 percentage points). In reality, Canada is currently forty-fourth in the world in terms of our contribution to peacekeeping and fourteenth among industrialized nations in terms of our contribution to overseas development assistance as a percentage of our gross national income (GNI), outranked by Norway, Sweden, Germany, Britain, and a host of others. The target of a foreign-aid contribution of 0.7 per cent of the GNI, accepted by the United Nations in 1969, was put forward by our very own Lester B. Pearson.

is high school. It is not a democracy! When I want you to have an opinion, I'll give it to you!" He wanted me to sit down and shut up, and his frustration, in view of the context, was arguably justified. But his attitude also speaks to the systematic way in which the thoughts, ideas, and contributions of youth are so frequently marginalized in society. Young people, in Canada and around the world, deserve to be listened to and to be engaged in meaningful ways in the political processes that shape and determine their lives. This world is on loan to us from our children, and from our children's children. *Notes from Canada's Young Activists* offers many powerful reasons to invest in those exceptional young people who not only promise to be the leaders of tomorrow but who are also, without question, the leaders of today. We have so much to learn from them, and it will be exciting to see where they go next. I know I, for one, will be watching and waiting with anticipation.

Samantha Nutt ("Sam") is a medical doctor and the Executive Director of War Child Canada, which she co-founded at the age of twenty-nine. War Child Canada is a registered charity that works in war-torn communities around the world, providing support to thousands of children and their families. Sam was chosen by Maclean's *magazine for their annual Honour Roll (celebrating twelve Canadians "making a difference"), was named one of Canada's Top 40 Under 40, and was profiled by* Flare *magazine as one of thirty "most outstanding Canadian women." She has been featured by* Time *magazine as one of Canada's five leading activists and, in 2006, was chosen by* Chatelaine *readers as one of twelve Canadian women they would most like to see run for politics. She lives with her husband and two-year-old son in Toronto. She writes frequently and speaks publicly on the global impact of war. For more information visit www.warchild.ca.*

Severn Cullis-Suzuki,
Kris Frederickson,
Ahmed Kayssi, and
Cynthia Mackenzie

W E'RE CALLED MEMBERS of Generation Y, the MTV Generation, the Twixter or Boomerang Generation. We grew
up with access to the world: through TV, travel, toys
made on the other side of the globe, the Internet. And although
we could watch wars as they happened around the world on
the news, in Canada we grew up in a time of peace and a lot of
prosperity. We can't imagine a time of economic depression,
world wars, or legal racial segregation.

But with the fruits of globalization came an unease. We
became expert consumers before we even got to school; we
were programmed by TV to *want* at an early age. We learned
about the hole in the ozone, then AIDS, then climate change.
While we learned that democracy was a Western gift to the
world, we also learned to despise our own politicians. And
now, though we live in one of the wealthiest nations in the

| 1

world, a collective anxiety manifests itself in stress, depression, ADD, loneliness, obesity, anorexia, and apathy. We have unprecedented access to media of all forms, but the doomsday messages they feed us are more than enough to make us put our blinders on, make us cynical or hopeless, or just turn us into hipsters.

But we are adapting—and evolving. Many among our generation have found a way to navigate the overwhelming deluge of information and use their tools to shift the status quo: Lyndsay Poaps, a pink-haired youth activist who ran for city office; Tim Harvey, who rowed across the Bering Sea to draw attention to our addiction to fossil fuel; Annahid Dashtgard, who decided to help her peers deal with their eating disorders; and Shakil Choudhury, who tackled his discomfort with his own heritage to promote racial tolerance. Someone forgot to tell them there was nothing they could do.

They are some of the inspiring young people whose personal stories moved the four of us and made us think about our own roles in the world. We, the editors of this collection, met through the Action Canada program, a fellowship with the idealist mandate of "building leadership for Canada's future." Thrown together, we began digging deeper beyond *what* we did to discover the motivations behind our work and our action: Why was Kris passionate about water and Aboriginal issues? Why was Cynthia dedicated to social equity and understanding policy and politics? Why was Severn passionate about the relationship between culture and ecology? Why was Ahmed driven towards politics and civic involvement (and why did he call himself KC)? It was our stories—not our CVs—that communicated who we really were.

Soon we were talking about people we knew with similar aims who were pushing for social change in a spectrum of ways—from the performance arts to politics to business. George Roter used his engineering training and gregarious personality to start Engineers Without Borders. Ilona Dougherty harnessed her social skills to bring rock stars, politicians, and young voters together. Miali-Elise Coley travelled the world to fight for her traditional way of life in the Arctic. We suddenly realized there was a vast network of young people who were building a nation they believe in and who, in changing their lives, are changing our worlds. These people apparently ignored the myths we are commonly taught: that we must choose between making a living and making a difference, between being respected and being effective, between pursuing a personal career and building a strong community. Instead, they were doing all of the above. It was surprising, and it was totally uplifting.

That conversation was the seed of this group of stories. We asked Daniel Aldana Cohen, a young writer who believes in the power of language to effect political change, to come on board and help us tell our tales.

In the midnight sun of the Yukon at our last Action Canada meeting, a social worker told us, "You can change someone's mind, but they can change it again. Change someone's heart, and that is forever." When we listen to Devi Mucina's stories of being a kid sleeping in a wastepaper bin in the midst of chaos in Harare, suddenly the issues of civil war in Africa are real. When we imagine what it was like for KC to vote as an Iraqi-Canadian, a country that hadn't held elections in fifty years, the concept of democracy takes on a different meaning. When we read how Anil Patel's life was changed with an accident that immobilized him for five months at thirteen, we can recognize the urgency of figuring out what is really important. Stories are the way that our hearts connect information to human meaning. Storytelling is our oldest form of communicating, and amid the drone of sound bites and media clips, it is still the most effective.

So here are stories of a world we can believe in. These people have shared with us their turning points, when something clicked inside that shifted how they recognized their responsibility in the world. Why did they act? Their stories are the explanation. Their catalysts for acting are all different. Their backgrounds are different. Their perspectives on the country are different. And so emerges one of the main messages of our book: *diversity* is the key to human survival and sustainability; no one "silver bullet" exists—solutions to our problems are many.

Some of these young activists, like Craig Kielburger, who founded Free The Children to end child labour, have devoted their energy to starting organizations that fight for social equity; others, like Jessica Lax and Natalie Gerum, are using the habits and attitudes of their daily lives to make fundamental shifts in social norms. Some, like Yuill Herbert, are using their voices to challenge governments to make important policy changes; others, like Ginger Gosnell-Myers, run for political positions and try to change government from within. Robin Rix and Chris Richards lent their efforts to work abroad; Richard Hoshino and Simon Jackson found their work at home in Canada.

Although their stories are diverse, they share themes of a sustainable, secure, and just future. They all reject the idea that nothing needs to be done and that nothing can be done. Their endeavours are rooted in idealism, but their actions show that their solutions are practical and achievable by all. They prove it's not naive to stand up for something—in fact, doing so has opened doors for them beyond anything they'd expected. Their success dares us to follow our dreams for the world.

They have struggled too—depression, guilt, and burn-out are a few of the afflictions along the path that follows the heart. Their journeys were as much about questioning their own identities as about shifting society. They have shared some of the personal challenges that accompanied their push against the norm.

In an age of unprecedented access to travel, several contributors had epiphanies on the other side of the planet that taught them to appreciate the ground beneath their feet. Cross-border organizations like Karen Kun's Waterlution and Ben Peterson's Journalists for Human Rights, and creative activism like d'bi. young's dub poetry, reflect a globalized reality that is normal to us. The contributors in this volume show us that when we stitch our global and local identities together, we can find the sustainable social and environmental solutions that seem so elusive.

As you absorb these stories, maybe you'll feel as we did reading them that anything *is* possible. We have designed the book so that it doesn't matter where you begin: peruse the stories in order, pick out the ones that catch your attention, or start reading simply where the pages fall open. How you choose to let the narrative affect you is the interesting part. If somewhere in this little pile of words you are moved by someone's action, hang on to that feeling—because you too are part of a web of Canadians and global citizens whose actions are changing the world. What kind of change that is, however, is entirely up to you.

ART, POLITICS,
AND QUESTIONING
AUTHORITY

Ilona Dougherty

■ ■ ■

WHAT DO YOU *want to be when you grow up? ALIVE.* I carried
this slogan on my placard protesting nuclear arms pro-
liferation. It was my first protest. I was three years old.
My family always encouraged me to challenge ideas in the
world around me. When I was in kindergarten my mom sent
me to school with a T-shirt that boldly commanded, "Question
Authority." At the same time, my parents worked hard to make
sure my brother and I understood that it was important to contribute to our global community. Indeed, my life's day-to-day
reality was global. My dad worked in Latin America with families like ours, and Latin American refugees would stay in our
house during their first days in Canada. Others stayed with us
too. One time, I learned that a guest who'd stayed with us a few
days earlier—a priest from Zimbabwe—was severely injured by
a letter bomb when he returned to his home country.

By fourteen I was a self-declared activist. I was always the odd one out in junior high: while other kids watched TV after school, I planned conferences and protests. There was always something to be done, a real sense of urgency. I learned the ins and outs of the activist community—I put in long hours, pulled all-nighters, and was never able to accomplish everything that needed to get done. On the flip side I discovered a sense of community with a group of people who were passionate about making positive change in the world.

My interest in social issues was complemented by a fervent passion for the arts. I'd taken dance classes since I was a little girl, but when I was fourteen I was diagnosed with fibromyalgia, a chronic illness that meant I would have to deal with intense muscle pain every day for the rest of my life. Because of my condition I had to take a step back from dance, but my love of the arts never left me, and it was that passion that would change my outlook.

When I was seventeen I was invited to participate as a youth delegate at the United Nations Commission on Sustainable Development. I was overwhelmed by the responsibility and the very concept of being at the UN. Wasn't the UN where the world came together to make things better? Where people put aside their differences to work side by side? But when I got there, I found a giant bureaucracy with a huge amount of paper waste, dusty, empty hallways, and a lot of bored-looking people. I was hoping to be inspired by my time there, to have my voice heard, to make a difference. But the only result of my two weeks on the UN delegation was two words included in the official documents: "youth" and "education." I suggested those two words be added and sat by the main negotiator through many of the sessions to make sure they got in. Important as those words are, however, the impact I had seemed so minute it was hard to justify all the time and energy I had put into being there. I left feeling that I had only been there for a photo op. It was a nice picture to have youth involved, but when it really came down to it, we weren't making the decisions, because all the decisions were being made in backrooms. Not the kind of change I imagined. And definitely not inspiring.

Disillusioned and conflicted, I started to re-evaluate the function of the activist community. What was effective about our work? And how could we be more effective? I began to question what really inspired me—if it wasn't the United Nations, then what was it?

From the bright lights of New York, I went back to my hometown of Whitehorse and back to grade twelve. For our upcoming graduation I organized a school talent show. At the event, one of the acts was a punk band called SOL whose energy and drive captured my imagination. They were just a local punk band like any other, but their energy was infectious. After the frustration I'd experienced at the UN, I was look-ing for a different, more creative way to reach people, and this band offered me just such an opportunity. I started working with them, and we produced a CD and booked shows. The skills I'd learned as an activist translated easily into working with artists. But the two worlds were so different—these musicians could get kids out to the shows; it wasn't a *struggle* to get peo-ple to show up and to listen. The five guys in the band brought loud music and the constant sense that *something* was about to happen. Their passionate, raw energy and their willingness to put everything on the line were addictive.

I'd found a creativity that the activist community lacked. I saw just how much music could affect people and make them feel strongly about something. Eliciting this kind of enthu-siasm was something my fellow activists weren't that good at. They were adept at talking to politicians and reaching out to people who already cared, but they couldn't seem to reach youth who didn't already know about the issues. I realized that art could speak to that audience. If we could blend the accessibility and emotional hook of art with the passion and conviction of my activist colleagues, then I felt that positive things would start happening—that we could both inspire and activate.

After high school I set this theory into motion. I had managed my health enough that, despite the pain, I was able to dance again, so I auditioned for a contemporary dance program at Concordia University in Montreal. Alongside my dance degree I also pursued a major in community affairs and policy studies. Everyone thought it was a bit strange that my interests were so diverse, but for me it was the perfect mix of art and action.

The year after I finished my degree at Concordia, I co-founded Apathy is Boring. Based in Montreal, Apathy is Boring uses art, media, and technology to engage youth in the democratic process. This project allows me to actualize both my artistic and activist sides every day. All three of the co-founders of Apathy is Boring are practising artists: Paul Shore is a filmmaker, Mackenzie Duncan is a photographer, and I continue to work as a modern dance choreographer.

Youth in Canada are disengaged from the political system. We don't trust politicians, only 36 per cent of us went out to vote in the 2006 election, and the number of youth who volunteer in their communities keeps shrinking. Apathy is Boring works with musicians, celebrities, and political parties to create forums that break down the barriers between youth and political leaders. We're breaking the rules about who has access to people with power. The formula is simple: put young people somewhere they feel comfortable—like a concert or online—bring politicians there, and see what happens.

At a concert we held in February 2005, we brought together Euphrates, an Iraqi hip hop emcee, a Conservative Member of Parliament, and a Green Party representative. It could have been a recipe for disaster, but the respect they offered one another when they shared the stage was amazing. The night ended up with a chilled-out vibe: everyone mingled and got to know where the others were coming from. Everyone was surprised at the dialogue we were able to generate, and the event really represented what Apathy is Boring is trying to accomplish.

Apathy is Boring challenges institutions like the Canadian government and the United Nations to really listen to what young people have to say. I don't want other youth to have the same kind of experience I had at the United Nations, so I work through Apathy is Boring to consult with government on how to become more youth-friendly. At the same time we reach out to young people to show them where they have the opportunity to be heard.

So far our work has been well received. Over our first two years we've been able to reach about 500,000 young people. We've run two successful "get out the vote" campaigns during federal elections, which included a public service announcement that ran in major movie theatres across the country for a week, media appearances on every channel from MuchMusic to CBC Newsworld, and a website that showcased quotes from musicians like Buck 65 and Melissa Auf der Maur alongside resources like a voting how-to guide. These are just some examples of how we're transcending the worlds of art and politics and how we're using both to reach out to a young audience that was ignored by traditional activist groups.

Every day I re-evaluate the work I do as we explore new ways of engaging young people. I have contemplated using fashion as an outreach tool and pondered how far we can take the art before our message becomes too abstract. I'm always walking a fine line between art and activism, constantly rethinking where each has its place. As Apathy is Boring continues to build momentum and take on a life of its own, we keep working to find ways to turn our democratic traditions into living traditions that will change and adapt to facilitate wider participation. I appreciate the grandness of that challenge. I'm glad that the slogan I carried when I was three years old has been fulfilled: my spirit is totally alive, inspired, and passionate about making positive change in my community happen in artistic and unpredictable ways.

■ ■ ■ ■ ■

A CHILD PROTESTOR, youth activist, and punk band manager, Ilona Dougherty grew up in Saskatchewan and Yukon and now lives in Mon-

treal. At fourteen she was the chair of the Canadian Environmental Network's Youth Caucus, and later she served on the National Youth Roundtable on the Environment, Sierra Youth Coalition Executive Committee, and Sierra Club of Canada Board of Directors. In January 2004 Ilona co-founded Apathy is Boring (www.apathyisboring.com), where she is currently the executive director. She also continues to dance (www.actionthroughart.com), manage bands (www.qaproductions.ca), and create award-winning choreography.

A REFERENCE

LETTER TO REMEMBER

George Roter

I WAS SO NERVOUS that my stomach was churning for the first time in years. It was April of 2004, and I was wandering dazed through a cavernous new terminal in Toronto's Pearson Airport, waiting to board a plane to Zambia.

There I was, a confident social entrepreneur, four years after founding Engineers Without Borders (EWB)—a successful, if sometimes broke, organization with a growing membership and international operations. EWB has a simple vision: a world without extreme poverty. We strive towards this vision by helping people in rural Africa improve their lives. To accomplish this lofty goal we send volunteers, many of them engineers, to work with the staff of local partner organizations on projects that range from helping individual farmers grow more and higher-quality food to helping communities install water pumps and sanitation facilities.

| 13

Yet despite having sent volunteer after volunteer on over-seas placements, I myself had never travelled to a single country where we work. I hadn't shared tea with village elders in the oppressive heat of Mali, a country that straddles the Sahel and Sahara deserts. Nor had I spent time with a hoe in my hand, preparing the fields alongside farmers in Zambia, a country less known for its people than the Zambezi River and Victoria Falls. I'd never met the people we serve.

A week later I sat up in bed and stared out the window at the sun just peeking over the horizon. It was a Sunday morning, about six o'clock, and I realized I still hadn't confronted my anxiety. I'd spent the past seven days immersed in the bustle of the development industry, running back and forth between government offices and NGO compounds, all in Lusaka, Zambia's capital city. Sure, over stacks of briefing papers I'd had in-depth discussions with EWB members and other NGO workers about small-scale farmers, rural entrepreneurs, and the women who struggle every day for the sake of their children. But it was all so maddeningly abstract. I still hadn't *met* any of these people. I still hadn't met my boss.

MY PASSION TO work towards a more just world started when I was very young. My first memories of Toronto are of a dilapi-dated bachelor apartment my parents rented in the mid-1970s after packing everything they owned into a hatchback and driving down the 401 from Montreal. They settled in Toron-to's west end, where my mother began working as a cocktail waitress to pay the bills and my father started a small consult-ing business.

In 1984 my father ran in the federal election as an inde-pendent candidate. He campaigned to spread one message: he plastered an entire Toronto riding with black lawn signs printed with the words "Nuclear Disarmament" in large white block letters. And he campaigned while running his own business, while two teenagers from an abusive family were taking refuge in our house, and while my mother pursued her own dream of entertaining children by becoming a self-employed professional clown. Looking back at my early childhood I see examples of the values that spawned my passion for social change and my entrepreneurial spirit. My parents were my role models.

And then there was that all-important cup of coffee, over which I decided to translate my values into action. Ironically enough, I was at a coffee shop—Timothy's—in one of Toronto's poshest neighbourhoods. My good friend Parker and I were catching up for the first time in four months. We told stories of our respective cycling adventures, his in South America and mine in Europe. Then Parker asked me, "Do you remember that idea we had in undergrad, Engineers Without Borders?"

Suddenly excited, we started talking about an organization that would get Canadians involved in reducing poverty around the world. Within minutes, we'd borrowed a pen from the cashier and started scribbling our first business plan on a napkin. By the time Timothy's had closed and kicked us out, we'd both implicitly made a commitment to carry this idea through.

Initially we believed EWB should provide communities with simple technologies, like latrines, grain mills, and irrigation pumps, that could help people in developing countries meet their basic needs. Latrines could help stop the spread of disease; grain mills and irrigation pumps could help feed families and generate the extra income needed to pay for education and child care.

I knew Canadian engineers had the skills and knowledge to help design and install these tools. And I quickly discovered that many were eager to. Our first volunteers were university students—young, enthusiastic, and inexperienced. We thought the technologies were simple enough that even volunteers with limited expertise could make a substantial difference on the ground.

That was the model, until we started questioning ourselves.

When Parker returned from a stint in Ghana, a democratic West African nation that was a magnet for development workers, we talked about the northern communities he'd visited there. They were all remarkably similar. Between five hundred and one thousand people lived in them, mostly subsistence farmers who grew just enough on their parched land to feed their families. Money was scarce. So was fresh water—those communities were stocked with hand-pumps, but the devices had rusted and no longer worked.

I asked Parker to explain this vast supply of useless hand-pumps. It turned out that during the 1970s and '80s, teams of engineers from Western countries had travelled to the region to install wells and hand-pumps, inspired by a model similar to our own. They would spend half a day per village, testing the ground, drilling a borehole, and installing a hand-pump. They measured success by the number of working pumps they'd installed by the end of each day.

Villagers would use the pumps for a couple of years until, not unexpectedly, a valve would seize or a piston would break, and nobody in the village would know how to fix the foreign technology. There were no local, trained technicians they could summon. Villagers lost trust in the "white man's" technology and left the pumps to sit and rust.

We asked ourselves if our model would repeat the problems of the past. We pushed ourselves to learn more about what we were doing and find better ways of making a sustainable, lasting difference. We realized it was necessary to train our volunteers extensively here at home, before they left. And when they got to one of the African countries where we work, and after earning the trust of local partners over the course of one to two years, they would contribute to building local capacity—that is, they would use their expertise to improve the ability of our partner organizations to help communities long after our volunteers leave. In practice, this process could entail something as simple as teaching field workers how to use a spreadsheet to improve reporting processes, to something as complex as helping to plan, from scratch, a water, sanitation, and hygiene education program to reach 500,000 people country-wide.

Constant questioning of ourselves has become a core value of EWB. Early on it taught us that concentrating on the technology itself was not the solution, and it has allowed us to understand the wisdom of something one of our Ghanaian partners recently told us: "You should measure your success not by the number of hand-pumps, but by the number of skilled technicians you leave behind."

We'd learned that being motivated to live up to one's ideals and give back to the community isn't enough. EWB's numbers are impressive—over 250 volunteers overseas and over twenty thousand members in Canada—but it's our core values that define us. Every volunteer we send overseas has heard me talk about these values; I consider them the organization's calling card: focusing on people, not problems, openly questioning ourselves, being entrepreneurial, and most important of all, remembering to remain humble. Starting and sustaining an organization like EWB certainly requires a lot of self-confidence, but its success on the ground depends on an extraordinary amount of humility—the recognition that leadership is about service and the vast amount we must learn from others. This combination of self-propulsion and modesty is what I now call humble entrepreneurialism.

Yet, discovering the importance of being humble is a long way from truly experiencing it.

THAT SUNDAY MORNING in Lusaka I decided it was time to finally meet the people I was working for. I spread out a large map of Zambia on the floor and looked for the smallest town I could travel to in a day: Chisamba. I knew nothing about the place. I hitchhiked a ride there on the back of a pickup truck.

Since Zambians are very pious I decided my best bet to meet people on a Sunday would be the local church. There I was, a pale, naive Jewish Torontonian wandering through a small African village looking for a church service to crash. As I approached a large, baked-mud, thatch-roofed hut, the Chisamba Pentecostal Holiness Church, I caught the sound of melodious singing and rhythmic clapping. I ducked in the door. My attempt to remain invisible was laughable. Immediately becoming the special guest, I was quickly led through the pews—shin-high wooden planks, really—to take a front-row seat.

Mostly, though, we were on our feet. Two hours of singing and dancing were punctuated by vigorous sermons in the local dialect of Njanja; the other congregants passed me simultaneous English translations on scraps of paper. The unbelievable service ended with a sermon the congregation urged me to give. I was hesitant to start, but I gradually gained confidence as I wove my way through the story of Joseph and his coat of many colours and as the congregation encouraged me with enthusiastic shouts of "Amen!" after each sentence.

What happened afterwards made an even more profound impression on me. Eustace, a congregant who has since become a friend, invited me into the lives of the people of Chisamba.

Eustace allowed me to listen and learn about the people behind the statistics. Joseph, a farmer, told me about the challenges of feeding his family. He's just one of 314 million sub-Saharan Africans living on less than a dollar a day. I met Anne, whose son died before his fifth birthday. He's one of the 192 out of every 1,000 children in Zambia who die of a preventable illness before the age of five. I also met Kelvim, a young entrepreneur who saved up for years to buy a single computer and who now runs computer training courses from the town hall. I met Eustace's aunt, who has managed to organize okra farmers in the area to pool their crops for sale in Lusaka.

These people are innovating and working hard to find a path out of poverty and to make their lives more comfortable. These are the people I work for.

I told Eustace the essentials of my life and my work with EWB. But mostly I listened to him talk about his life. As the day was ending, I asked him a question, the answer to which I'll never forget.

"What do you dream of?"

"A better life for my children than I had."

I realized then how alike we were. We parted with a typically long African handshake.

Six weeks later, back in my pleasant Toronto office, I received a letter from Eustace. He'd spent a day's pay to send me a note, which ended, "Your humbleness really touched our community and changed my wrong perceptions about whites, especially those from the West. I want you to continue your work."

I didn't install a pump, train a technician, or help coordinate a local development initiative in Chisamba. But I did meet my boss. Face to face with the people EWB serves, I was profoundly humbled in a way I had so often spoken about but never truly *lived*. I finally fully grasped the core values that I espoused. And I have a letter of reference I carry with me everywhere.

■ ■ ■ ■ ■

GEORGE ROTER, a native of Toronto, Ontario, co-founded Engineers Without Borders (www.ewb.ca) with Parker Mitchell at the turn of the millennium. He was awarded an Action Canada Fellowship on public  policy in 2004 and in 2005 was named one of Canada's Top 40 Under 40.

BUILDING A NATION OF NATIONS: ABORIGINAL YOUTH AND CANADIAN POLITICS

Ginger Gosnell-Myers

I GREW UP WITH my mother and father, brothers and sisters. I had many aunties and uncles and over a hundred cousins, and we all lived together in an isolated village called New Aiyansh in the Nass Valley of northern British Columbia. Every summer I would accompany my fisherman father along the B.C. coast catching salmon, halibut, crabs, the odd octopus, snapper, and sometimes a shark or a seal. On days off we would anchor the boat along some pristine stretch of the coastline and row a smaller boat to the shore to pick berries and make a fire to roast marshmallows.

During the fall we would smoke, dry, and can sockeye salmon to get us through to the following year. My mom would can fruits and jams. We even canned clams, cockles, and the now-extinct abalone. We would prepare moose for the feasts and celebrations the village would hold over the seasons. We lived a traditional Nisga'a life with a modern twist. In school I learned the ABCs and 1-2-3s and how to speak Nisga'a. Our school was decorated with lava rocks from the time a nearby volcano exploded over five hundred years ago, and in front of the school was a totem pole with a man holding a rainbow at the top.

In the winter the temperature would drop below minus forty degrees. The snow would build quickly and sometimes top seven feet to cover the houses. When the snow receded we would find animals, like puppies and cats, frozen along our sidewalks and stuck inside blocks of ice that were too big to be chipped away at or melted. So we left them untouched through the season, and kids passing by would gawk at them.

In spring the bears would wake up from their hibernation, and the villages would be on grizzly alert. The Nisga'a territory is home to the largest population of grizzly bears in the world. When you drive into the Nisga'a valley to get to the villages you go past trees that are almost a thousand years old, rivers that are ice blue in the winter, and miles of lava rocks facing glacier-topped mountains. These childhood experiences defined and shaped me. When I think about what life should be like, I think about the life I once lived.

DURING MY FIRST year at Malaspina University-College in Nanaimo I met a lot of young people in the First Nation Studies program who quickly became my friends. Soon I was living in a house with four roommates, and all of their friends would stop by to visit, sometimes to study but usually to hang out. We would sit around our big house and talk about the complicated lives we left behind in our communities, the family and friends we missed, old crushes and new ones, and other gossip.

One time my household organized a traditional feast at the school for the other students in our program. The five of us planned a five-day road trip to gather Indian foods from our families back home. We picked up moose meat in Moricetown and then travelled to Prince Rupert for halibut, clams, salmon, seaweed, and herring roe. We wanted to collect the foods we loved and at the same time were excited for an excuse to see our friends and family again. The afternoon of the feast we performed the dances and stories from our nations and played Lahal, a gambling and guessing game in which two teams of six sit across from each other, specially designed bones are hidden in the hands of a few players, and a set of sticks is used to keep track of points. Each team must guess which hands on the opposing team hold the special bones. A correct guess wins the guessing team one stick, while an incorrect guess costs the team a stick, and the game is played until one team wins the other's entire set of sticks. There's a lot of singing, yelling, pointing, and body gestures to distract the guessing team.

After that successful event we extended our coordinating talents to organizing student potluck dinners and holiday parties at our home. We always worked towards creating a sense of community. Soon the school program that I was originally so excited about started to end, and so did my interest in the program itself. During the last two months of the term I tried to ignore the fact that I was neglecting school. I thought my friends had the same attitude towards school that I did, and they didn't seem to regret their behaviour. We were having a great time together, and we were always busy doing something social. But I never noticed that they were managing to complete their school work on top of all of their other commitments.

The day I picked up my final transcript I couldn't look at it for the first hour. I already felt like a failure and didn't want the proof. When I finally opened it I felt wrecked. My only course of action was to talk to the First Nations counsellor at the school; it was the first time I'd gone to him for advice. I never expected him to tell me that he also failed his first year of college, and his second year, and still managed eventually to pull himself together. He'd done a lot worse in his first year than I did in mine, and he wasn't a statistic sitting unemployed and uneducated living in the middle of nowhere. I'd always thought that students who failed a year would never succeed— that maybe they weren't meant to be good at school and were destined to move home to work at the local grocery store for the rest of their lives. That day I walked four hours from the college to the Nanaimo ferry terminal and hopped on the next boat to Vancouver; during that time I thought about the things I would have to do to get my life on track again. For those four hours I was my own cheerleader.

I didn't know what I wanted to do with my life at that point. I thought that by pursuing higher education I'd eventually have a career path, but I found myself neither educated nor on the road to gainful employment. The following year, when I started a new program at the Institute of Indigenous Government in Vancouver, I had to commit to being a working student while living off a small student loan. I think having to work extra hard to succeed and not wanting to let myself down again got me past that year. I really wanted to make a good life for myself. There's a saying that I always thought about: winners do things that losers don't do.

A FEW YEARS ago I decided to seek out and engage people who made the big decisions on how to run the country. I approached this new pursuit with a cautious curiosity, because I was unfamiliar with federal politics and how it could play a role in my life. I'd already been working as a youth advocate at the provincial and national levels, creating projects and writing policy for youth engagement, and I was looking for new opportunities to participate in decision-making processes. I wanted to reverse the appallingly archaic political decisions and eradicate the discriminatory law enforcement that to this day are incredibly harmful to Aboriginal people.

One day a good friend invited me to a dinner hosted by the Liberal Party of Canada (LPC) in Vancouver. I didn't know what to expect of the evening, but I went because I knew that, at the very least, I would be in the company of my friend, would eat a good supper, and could learn something about the LPC. More than a thousand people attended that dinner, and the two of us sat in the back corner of the enormous and well-decorated room watching everyone dressed in business attire carry wine glasses, walk the room, and network. I, in contrast, felt glued to my seat and didn't venture from the table until it was time to leave.

Yet I remember seeing, in the distance, many First Nations leaders at a full table chatting with various cabinet ministers. I was surprised to see other Aboriginal people there at all. They looked like they were having a good time, and they socialized well with the crowd that evening. Until that night my knowledge of First Nations political activity was limited to the community level and involved only other Aboriginal peoples. Until that dinner I'd believed that there was no room for Aboriginal peoples outside of Aboriginal-specific politics.

I was so curious about the LPC after that evening that I decided to find out more about becoming active in a political party. A friend who was an LPC member told me that the party held the only designated space for people of First Nations ancestry to meet and work together on policies through the Aboriginal Peoples Commission (APC), which had a membership of over sixteen thousand Aboriginal individuals. I realized that joining the LPC would allow me to take my advocacy to the national level, with a federal party that I felt was working hard to actively include Aboriginal issues in its political agenda.

I'd always believed that one way of advocating youth involvement in decision making was to work in those positions in politics myself. I ran for a national executive position within the Aboriginal Peoples Commission along with a slate of three other young colleagues at the Liberal leadership convention in Toronto in 2003, and we won. We wanted to show everyone who felt that young people didn't deserve to be decision makers that we could and we would contribute to the political process.

In First Nations society being affiliated with a federal political party is equivalent to selling out. It's seen as helping to maintain the status quo for Aboriginal communities, and I grew up believing this viewpoint. But when I took steps to truly understand what federal politics entailed, I felt empowered. I ended up going against the norm and participating in partisan politics because I could see the value of being in a position where I can respectfully speak to, work with, and, I hope, influence people who run the country.

My biggest passion now is working on advancing Aboriginal rights in Canada and including youth in that process. The APC is one arena in which this work takes place: through the APC I've helped develop policies for youth leadership opportunities, and I've worked with other young people to lobby on behalf of Aboriginal causes at policy conventions.

I'd like to think that my actions and experiences—from my failures to my successes—show everyone what First Nations youth can achieve when they are included and respected. I give thanks and honour the opportunities I've had to become stronger, more humble, and more thoughtful. And as I remember the Nass Valley and all its powerful beauty, I promise myself to one day live again in a place I deeply love and believe in.

GINGER GOSNELL-MYERS is a B.C.-born member of the Nisga'a and Kwagiulth First Nations. She is an elected member of the Liberal Party of Canada's Aboriginal Peoples Commission National Executive (www.apc-cpa.ca), and she has worked with the First Nations Child and Family Caring Society (www.fncfcs.com), Urban Native Youth Association, and the Centre for Native Policy and Research (www.cnpr.ca). She is the former co-chair to the Assembly of First Nations National Youth Council, and she has addressed the United Nations Permanent Forum of Indigenous Peoples.

IT'S ABOUT TIME

Anil Patel

I HAVE BEEN IN pain for a long time. On February 12, 1988, during one of the worst snowstorms of the decade, my friend Stephanie's father was driving us home from swim practice on the two-lane highway between Peterborough and Lakefield, Ontario. A drunk driver's car ploughed into ours. Mr. Taylor died in the hospital. Stephanie was hurt, but not too badly. I suffered serious abdominal injuries and fractured my two lower vertebrae. The rest of the winter was a haze—I was in pain and overwhelmed by what had happened.

I spent three months recovering in the hospital. My routine was murderous: four hours on my back, four hours on my left side, and four hours on my right side, plus an injection of morphine at each "turning." Repeated twice daily. The bed sores got bad, the nightmares worse. Next came two months of bedrest at home. I spent the summer in a full-length back brace until the healing was complete. Mum, who rarely left my side, was my saviour.

Despite the successful recovery process, the doctors warned me I'd face painful complications as I got older. They were right. I think it's safe to say I haven't had a pain-free day in seventeen years. In 2001 one of my disks slipped, and in 2003 it slipped twice more. Each time I was confined to three weeks' bedrest. Losing my ability to be productive was devastating: I was busy with work and school and found myself exhausted and unable to do anything. Mum's death made the situation even harder to bear.

Frances Marion Patel passed away on November 27, 2000, at the age of fifty-two. The illness was a rare form of aggressive cancer; it was painful, and it was swift. As I worked through the pain of losing her, I focused on my bright memory of who she was and what she contributed to forming my ideas and my sense of responsibility.

My mum was a role model and community leader in our town, Chatham, Ontario. She was active in everything and especially encouraged us to share in her love of sport. She began as a volunteer on the deck of almost every regional swim meet my siblings and I participated in. She went on to become president of our local swim club, a volunteer position she held for several years. But her real passion was tennis. She got us to pick up the raquet and hit the courts in Chatham. When she realized the junior tennis program we were enrolled in was floundering, she decided to fix it by becoming its director. During her tenure, participation in the program grew to record numbers. Then she became president of the tennis club. Like many parents who support their kids unconditionally in competitive sports, she sacrificed a lot of her time, energy, and social life during our formative years.

She was just as dedicated to helping others in her professional life. She worked in long-term care because she believed that our society has an obligation to take care of its elders. Once a month she drove from our home in Chatham, where she usually worked, to work for a week in Bourget, a small Franco-Ontarian town just outside Ottawa. She felt that helping an unacceptably run-down seniors' home in desperate need of dedicated staff was worth the 1,700-kilometre round trip.

I'd always known Mum was involved in community life, but I didn't fully understand how impressive her involvement was until she was gone. Not a day goes by that I don't miss her or appreciate the clarity she's given me through her life's example. I made a decision on the day she died that I'd direct my grief into something that would celebrate her memory—something to make her proud. I knew making this commitment would be the only way I could go on.

I remembered that when I was young, before my accident, I was involved the way other kids were. I followed the example of my active parents and drew strength from them—creative ideas from my dad, work ethic from my mum. But I had never taken the next step, never made my commitment to my community a fundamental part of my life.

Dealing with the sadness, frustration, and anger brought on by a parent's death isn't easy. When the physical pain of my recurrent back problems compounded my emotional pain, it was tempting to unleash my energy in destructive or selfish ways. Three weeks of immobility is a long time to stew. But lying there in bed as my slipped disks healed, I managed to get hold of myself. It wasn't easy, and it took a lot of discipline, but I was able to ball up this negative potential energy and push it in a positive direction, towards constructive action.

For some time, I'd become increasingly aware of Canada's lack of progress in many social and environmental areas. All the indicators were depressing: our health system was deteriorating, homelessness was up, pollution was intensifying—it seemed that everywhere our standard of living was stubbornly falling. There were so many causes that needed help that I had trouble deciding where to invest my energy.

At first I decided to volunteer for an existing charity. I researched the programs of about twenty organizations. Of the twenty, I contacted ten whose programs I really liked. Of those, only three got back to me. One organization lost my résumé twice. This same organization forgot I was scheduled to come in for an orientation. The administrative assistant (also the unofficial volunteer coordinator) had no idea what to do with me, so she hastily asked if I could clean the vermin compost bin under the sink. I did, but that first day was also my last.

I assumed getting involved would be simpler. Looking back, I had an easier time finding a job than a volunteer opportunity. Although I did eventually find a good match, I'd learned an important lesson—one that was confirmed by my broader research into the voluntary sector and the problems it was meant to address.

I discovered that what Canada's non-profit and voluntary organizations had in common was the underdevelopment of their resources, skills, and strategies to engage, train, and retain volunteers. There are over 6.5 million active volunteers in Canada, but a tiny proportion is doing the bulk of the work. My own generation's involvement was unacceptably weak. Fewer and fewer young people, I found, were putting in their volunteer hours. It became clear to me that what Canada needed was an initiative to strengthen its volunteer infrastructure, to encourage young Canadians to take up volunteerism, and to make it easier for them to do so.

In 2001 three university friends—Simon Foster, Mick Maiese, and Andrew Klingel—and I co-founded Framework

Foundation to address our generation's disengagement. This new project was a wonderful transition from drinking beer and eating pizza together to building strategic plans to engage our peers in getting involved with their community. Our organization's call to action—an extension of our own coming together on this project—is, "It's time for you to get in the picture." We don't distribute money but, rather, time: the most valuable commodity any of us possesses.

We host our call to action through a first-of-its-kind event, a Timeraiser. A Timeraiser is a silent art auction with a twist: you bid volunteer time (either in your professional capacity or as a pair of hands) to one of our partner volunteer organizations. Winning participants have twelve months to complete their pledge to receive their art, a reminder of their goodwill. The art isn't donated, though. Framework Foundation raises money from the corporate sector to purchase art from artists, since we believe that investing in our nation's cultural community is vital.

This event is targeted at young people, aged twenty-two to thirty-five. This peer-to-peer model means that we're working with people who are at the same stage in their lives as us and who are dealing with similar issues. We know who we're working with and how to reach them. This understanding has been key to our hosting two successful Timeraisers, which have generated thousands of volunteer hours and supported dozens of volunteer agencies. We're currently planning two more, and these events are just the beginning.

32 | Our broader goal is to redefine the role of volunteerism in the lives of young Canadians. We worry that as it stands, volunteerism is just a marginal part of "life" in the typical "work–life" balancing act. A recent visit to Winnipeg cast light on this issue. Some friends and I met with Aboriginal leaders to

explore the idea of having non-Aboriginals volunteer at non-profit organizations serving the Aboriginal community, thus building bridges on the ground between the two communities.

We were surprised to be told that the term "volunteerism" doesn't translate into most First Nations, Métis, or Inuit languages. The closest translation is "giving and sharing." It's such a fundamental aspect of Aboriginal culture that it's not compartmentalized the way it is for non-Aboriginals. I think that's the same lesson, ultimately, that I came to learn from my mum, though until my meeting with the Aboriginal leaders I'd never been able to articulate it. When volunteerism and community building become the very foundation on which we live our lives, then the real, positive change happens that can move us towards lasting, deep, sustainable development.

Putting this insight into practice has been a difficult journey. I sometimes have a hard time explaining to myself what I'm doing here. I haven't seen much of my family or friends over the past three years. I knew from the start that founding a charity while going to school wouldn't be easy—or cheap. But ultimately I couldn't in good conscience choose to do anything else. Once I could clearly see, and deeply feel, how much needs to be done and how much young Canadians can contribute if only they're mobilized, I had to take action. I owed it to my mum, and I owed it to myself.

Besides, I've been rewarded for my sacrifices—I have hope again. I now have a recurring dream, which is dramatically different from the nightmares I had for months in the hospital after my accident. Now, when I close my eyes, I find myself in the not-so-distant future. Here's what I see: The number of volunteers has been increasing year after year. People taking action are solving problems and strengthening our communities. Front-line volunteer organizations working effectively and efficiently are fuelling the change. Headlines around the world read that the spirit—and definition—of being actively engaged is changing. As young Canadians discover that balancing their lives means giving as much as they take, they're transforming their country.

■ ■ ■ ■ ■

ANIL PATEL has been a volunteer for many years and is a founding member of the Framework Foundation. He is also a volunteer with

United Way of Toronto and BoardMatch. In the future he hopes to travel to all corners of Canada—plus many points in between.

Severn Cullis-Suzuki

I SIT ON THE edge of the world. It's my favourite spot, the rock of Quadra Island slipping into the Pacific Ocean. I look across at the familiar peaks of B.C.'s Coast Mountains. I've looked across at them since I was eight. Today I'm twenty-five. This weekend the family cabin is full of friends—Sue, Mandeep, Dennis, Kym, Lorne, Carla, and D. Wong. On the beach this morning at low tide, I watched my friends turn into children as we collected oysters and dug for clams. I shared their reactions and felt the wonder of gathering this food from the land. It *is* so amazing when you think about it—amazing that we can collect food right from the mud on the beach. But besides the fact that this beach feeds us every time we come up here and that it holds an incredible wealth of biodiversity, I had never really thought too much else about this stretch of sand and shells. Last year I was told a story that profoundly shifted the way that I look at this land and how I see myself on it.

In my ethnoecology class a guest speaker from the Qualicum First Nation, Chief Kim Recalma-Clutesi, told us the story of the clam gardens. Several years ago John Harper, a geomorphologist surveying for the government, flew over the beaches of Vancouver Island at a zero-level tide and noticed strange semicircles of bowling ball–sized rocks on the beaches. He couldn't tell whether they were natural or human-made. During the survey he saw hundreds of them up and down the coast of the Island. It took him nine years of searching for their cause to finally get in touch with Kwakxistala, Clan Chief Adam Dick, a Kwakwaka'wakw elder who knew exactly what they were: *luxiways*. The *luxiways* are the long-forgotten clam gardens, rock terraces that the Kwakwaka'wakw people built for optimum clam growth. After our government's efforts to denounce, assimilate, and forget the traditions of this country's original peoples, no one spoke of them. The beaches were left unused, but the rocks remained. Archaeological digs show that clams became a main food in the Broughton Archipelago about two thousand years ago, suggesting that's when the technology for the clam plateaus began to expand on this coast.

Having grown up in a household that was somewhat pessimistic about environmental issues, I had always thought that human presence automatically meant the extinction of natural resources. But this story of clam gardens painted a different picture. Not only did humans on the West Coast practise sustainable harvesting, but they actually practised sustainable aquaculture that supported high population densities around the north end of Vancouver Island. I had lived on the coast my whole life and never knew about these methods and traditions. For me, this discovery was incredible. I sat there in class, staring at photographs of the rocky beaches, totally absorbed, when suddenly it dawned on me that the beach that has sustained my family with clams for seventeen years on Quadra Island was one of these clam gardens, a *luxiway*.

Today as my friends dug clams I looked at the rock formation and couldn't believe I'd never seen it before. There is an obvious ledge of bowling ball–sized rocks that guards the sandbar stretching across the beach. It is evidence of the human use of this land for two thousand years, and the fact that it still provides us with an abundance of clams tells a story of care, calculation, and sustainability. And suddenly, my identity in this scene has shifted: I am no longer just an individual who digs clams on the beach. Suddenly, by knowing that two thousand years of hands and bellies and minds used and maintained this beach, I am part of a continuum—I now have the responsibility to pass it on to two thousand more years of clam eaters.

In the city, our connection to land, our sense of responsibility to our land and our community, and our sense of being part of a continuum in history, are invisible. We float as individuals living individual moments in history and time. We don't think about the fact that we're the ancestors of future generations. Mom dropped a profound statement on me the other day: "More and more I have this sense of being an ancestor . . . " I am an ancestor, too. Over food in downtown Toronto, poet and hip hop artist K'Naan told me about *Ab Tiris*, a Somali term for the recitation of the names of one's father, father's father, and so on. He says he can recite his forefathers' names back two thousand years. I can recite back two fathers. I try to fathom how his awareness of his ancestry affects his sense of who he is, what his role is in the continuum of his own history and the history of his people, and what he's here to do. Perhaps the closest understanding I can relate is my awareness, standing on the beach today, of being one in a long line of clam diggers using this beach for food.

As I show one of my friends how to slice the muscle joining the shells of an oyster we collected, she asks, "Aren't we hurting them?" We're killing these animals to eat them. I give thanks as we do it. My mind automatically flashes back to my auntie Diane showing me how to clean and work on fish in Skidegate one summer when one of Chief Dempsey Collinson's boats full of salmon came in. She taught me that you have to give thanks as you cut the fish and that you can't think negative or disrespectful thoughts. It's almost ceremonial. That day I butchered many spring salmon and learned how to clean fish and give thanks. When we catch and kill our own food, or grow it, we clean it differently, eat it differently, digest it differently. I wonder how it nourishes our bodies differently.

Here on Quadra everyone in our little posse is involved in the food-collecting and preparing process this whole weekend, and I notice how quickly ceremony develops—candles are lit, wine is poured, and finally we all sit down together; toasts happen and suddenly taking care and time and enjoyment in celebrating these precious moments is the most important, human thing we could possibly be doing.

This is so enjoyable! I wonder, Why don't we always sit together, eat together, give thanks together? This kind of event is not something only the wealthy, or the humble, can partake in. It is something innately human and natural to all of us.

Since I was a little kid I've believed that I make a difference in the world, and that difference, I decided, had better be positive. I started by forming an environmental club with my friends, and we ended up speaking to world leaders at the UN, asking them to remember their children when they made their decisions about environment and development.

Since then I've been to many more conferences, and my experiences have altered what I think can "change the world." I think about some of the ways I've pushed for change—marching in protest against the oppression of the IMF or in solidarity with the landless people's movement in Johannesburg, speaking my mind to the Hornby Island Community Centre and the Nike Corporation about the rights of youth and the inseparability of social and ecological perspectives, biking across Canada to remind people they shouldn't tolerate air pollution. I have encouraged young people—all people—to speak out about what they care about and what they know is wrong. And I often wonder, what is "radical"? Is it speaking to world politicians? Is it protesting the WTO or the FTAA? Is it starting a business with a triple bottom line of social, environmental, and corporate responsibility? Is it paying attention to the effects of our small actions? It is *all* of these things.

But, beyond using my voice in the world, I also feel radical right here: sitting down to food I collected from the land and prepared with friends, in a world that most of the time pushes me to do the opposite. I look at my friends around me and see people who are often reminded of the sadness of the world's shrinking diversity, people who resent that each of us is complicit, though we never agreed to making an inherent contribution to ecological or social destruction. I see in us all people who crave emancipation from apathy, for something tangible to free us from cynicism, something to counter the guilt and sadness that comes with being aware...

So here we are at the table. In a media cacophony of desperate global statistics on ecological and cultural destruction, one of our most important, real tasks is to *appreciate* what we have, to never take it for granted, and to seek out the connections that ground us to the beautiful responsibilities that come with being human. We can sink roots down into the land; we can make a commitment to what *belonging* somewhere means. We can figure out what we believe in, and then we can stand up and speak out about those beliefs. We can recognize and reach towards the First Peoples who are still here, because our Canadian history and destiny is inextricably linked with theirs. Identifying our connections to each other, to the land, to our past, to our own selves and identity in this world, is one of the most important conversations we can have right now, as we ancestors decide what we want life to be about for the next two thousand years.

Our own ancestors come from around the planet, but tonight on Quadra Island we sit down to a clam feast on Kwakwaka'wakw territory. We give thanks for the oysters and the ancestors whose foresight feeds our bellies, and we will do our best to honour our role in the great continuum.

■ ■ ■ ■ ■

SEVERN CULLIS-SUZUKI has been speaking out on social justice and environmental issues since she was small. She founded the Environmental Children's Organization at age nine and attended the Rio Earth Summit in 1992 and several UN summits since. She is a commissioner for the Earth Charter and spearheaded the "Recognition of Responsibility," taking it to the Johannesburg Summit in 2002 and on tour in Japan. She has a B.Sc. in biology from Yale and is currently studying ethnoecology at the University of Victoria with traditional Kwakwaka'wakw elders on the West Coast where she grew up.

Karen Kun

I SHIVERED AS I crawled out of my sleeping bag at six in the morning on the day my life changed. It was the summer of 1999, and I was living in a small house in rural Costa Rica, where I was doing development work with a Canadian NGO. My job that day was to hike for an hour to go help some farmers and small businesses slaughter chickens for market.

As I walked along the narrowing paths through the lush, green jungle I found myself asking questions I'd never considered before: What was my real, *lasting* contribution to this community? Weren't the local people just as capable of doing the work as I was? I hadn't avoided these questions on purpose. I'd simply been blinded by my romantic illusions about development work: of living in a jungle with real Costa Ricans, waking up to monkeys howling in the morning, and eating strange local food.

That morning, as my illusions dissipated, I started to panic about my job. I worked with some of the country's poorest people but was regularly invited to socialize in wealthy Costa Rican and expatriate society. This contrast gave me a deep respect for my indigenous friends' lifestyles, values, and connection to their land. But it also made me realize how profoundly I'd tricked myself into believing I could appear out of thin air and with my expertise solve all their problems. After my walk in the jungle I decided to leave the country—and never to work formally in the developing world again.

It was time to come home to my own country. Although working in Costa Rica—as well as Bolivia and Colombia before that—had been an extraordinarily positive experience, one where I learned an incredible amount, forged some of my deepest friendships, and came to love passionately the communities where I worked, I needed to be in the place where my commitment was deeply rooted—somewhere I'd never leave if the going got tough.

In the months after my resignation I faced a lot of criticism. Friends in Costa Rica and Canada said that I'd have a negative mark on my employment record forever and that I was a fool to walk away from a position I'd worked so hard to earn. I worried that they were right, but I fundamentally felt that by living in Latin America I was not pursuing my long-term vision, although I had yet to discover what that vision would be.

One day a Colombian friend asked me what I'd want to show her if she came to Canada to visit. I thought about it for a moment and told her I'd take her to see Lake Ontario, maybe with a visit to Niagara Falls, a canoe trip, or a hike through the Niagara escarpment. She laughed and said, "Karen, you love water, don't you?"

At that point I consciously realized for the first time the deep significance water had always had in my life. Bodies of water always calmed me down. I think clearly when I'm listening to the rush of a river or staring at my reflection in the blue surface of a lake. I turn to water when I need to contemplate my career or a romantic relationship, gather my thoughts, or gain reassurance to spur me forward over life's big hurdles. I grew up five hundred metres from the edge of Lake Ontario and often spent time there with my family, but it only occurred to me as I spoke with my friend that I needed to live near a vast body of water for my spiritual, emotional, and intellectual well-being. I feel uneasy when water is not nearby.

Latin Americans can always come up with a story about the importance of water. In many villages the river is at the very heart of community life. I especially like that a river bank is the main "dating" locale in a lot of rural areas. Young boys helping their mothers collect clean drinking water would catch glimpses of young girls cleaning pots or doing laundry and form crushes that matured as they grew up. An elderly man in Bolivia once told me, "If it weren't for that little river, I would never have known my wife." Such stories are harder to find in Canada, and I know that most Canadians fail to appreciate the enormous importance of water to our existence.

My curiosity about water-related issues grew, and I took a series of advanced geography courses on water systems at York University. I also started to think about how to achieve true social and environmental sustainability and realized that change begins in the community, so I became involved in local initiatives: I joined gardening groups, became active in Food-Share programs, and volunteered on municipal political campaigns. It occurred to me while I was in Costa Rica that my ability to fundamentally change the way people lived their lives was limited in a country that was not my own, and if I was going to make an indelible imprint on the way a society engages with its environment, I would have to start in my own backyard. I felt that in Canada our understanding of the way our environment influences every aspect of our society was still underdeveloped. Incredibly, most Canadians can't name the source of the water running through their household taps.

I decided to start an organization that would fuse my passions for water and community. I knew it would be rooted in Canada but would connect to people around the world with expertise in community development. I knew this endeavour would be a long-term project, but I still had no idea what shape this organization would take.

In August of 2002 I attended the World Summit on Sustainable Development in Johannesburg, South Africa. As I took in the sessions about biodiversity, forestry, green energy, and sustainability and interacted with the other delegates, I started to understand the extent of our dependence on water: developing countries cannot be helped if their people can't access clean water; water is the backbone of many renewable energy initiatives; water shortages may lead to water resources being privatized. And then, like an ice-cold shower, the epiphany jolted me awake: *nothing* is sustainable if people don't consider the entire water system. Water affects every part of our environment and our society, and without it, none of the world's ecosystems or industries—from resource extraction to manufacturing—could survive. I knew that I had to focus on water and that it was time to take action. One year later, Waterlution was born.

I co-founded Waterlution with Tatiana Glad, a very close friend who shared my vision of creating dialogue that fostered a reverence for water and its influence on the planet. Waterlution's fundamental goals would be to inspire people to embrace their connection with water and to challenge them to consider its importance in every decision they make. We wanted Waterlution to prompt people to find long-term solutions for water pollution, shortages, and overuse. We aimed to bring people together and encourage them to look at their common inextricable link to water. And because each person would understand this link in a unique way, whether aesthetically, spiritually, or pragmatically, we decided Waterlution's programs would be experiential, without a set curriculum, and would be carried along by the participants and not by our own agenda.

To fulfill our mandate we've had to be flexible and innovative, and we made sure we had a presence in communities, the business and industrial sectors, and all levels of government. To connect with a wide spectrum of people we have pursued diverse creative avenues: we run small-scale workshops and learning journeys—experiential explorations of the different roles water plays in society—to deepen our society's understanding of water systems; we have made films, including, most recently, *The New Culture of Water*, which we shot in South Africa; we have a partnership with *Corporate Knights* magazine, a Canadian publication dedicated to promoting business practices that are socially and environmentally responsible and that foster empathy, compassion, and respect in the marketplace; and we publish newsletters several times a year. We have worked to reach a wide audience with our message—for example, we conduct workshops in public schools for free, using the fees we charge private schools for the same workshop to cover the costs—and although we're committed to remaining grounded in Canada, water systems are global, so we keep a large international network of friends and colleagues, including the members of Pioneers of Change and other groups of social entrepreneurs, to share expertise and support each other's projects.

Waterlution takes a concrete, practical approach in its programs. We take children on field trips to see the water system

45

in action—for example, to rivers or water purification plants. And our workshops are interactive: the participants share impressions, questions, and viewpoints with one another to discover their own relationships to water. We focus on developing deep, genuine dialogue between individuals by taking them on our learning journeys, which put them physically in some of the places—including factories, businesses, parks, and just about everywhere in between—in which water plays a pivotal role.

Through these methods we expose people to different ideas, make them think, encourage them to interact, and inspire them to keep learning. I've even shown incredulous bankers that their profession has deep connections to water: their myriad published reports depend on pulp and paper manufacturers, industries known to pollute the many rivers and watersheds of southern Ontario. These manufacturers are in turn connected to forestry companies that use vast water resources to transport and clean logs. Meanwhile the investment sector and stock markets represent a community of industries—transports, fisheries, agriculture, waste disposal, et cetera—totally dependent on fresh- or saltwater systems. Waterlution works to highlight these many connections, and the majority of the people and organizations we have worked with tell us that they feel inspired by the connections they make through our programs.

Getting Waterlution off the ground was hard work. When Tatiana and I began, we followed up on every lead and tried to make contact with as many government representatives, business leaders, funders, volunteers, and workshop participants as possible. We worked every day of the week to fundraise and develop our programs. To get everything done, I began to cut out friends, exercise, social activities. For two years I was running on adrenaline, like an extreme-sports addict, getting off on the rush of people being interested in what Waterlution was doing. It was so important to me that Waterlution last and be sustainable that I worked obsessively to ensure its survival by reaching out and promoting its cause. At times I hovered on the verge of burnout.

I've since learned that that pace isn't sustainable, and I've figured out how to spend time with the people close to me, how to give myself space to be spontaneous, how to take time off to pursue interests outside of Waterlution. I've seen many phenomenal social entrepreneurs who put in so much so fast they couldn't maintain their projects, and I'm determined not to become one of them. My new inner balance and Waterlution's sure footing have allowed me to take on a second big responsibility as publisher of *Corporate Knights*.

When we first started Waterlution Tatiana and I locked ourselves into an apartment in Zurich, Switzerland, for five days to hammer out Waterlution's principles, which include recognizing the interdependence of water and society, keeping a balance of action and reflection, being locally committed but globally aware, and bringing together diverse stakeholders as equal players in discussions about water. We check in with these principles regularly and refuse to do work that doesn't inspire us. It's essential to us that we continue evolving without diluting Waterlution by taking on projects that we don't consider meaningful. If Waterlution is to remain pure in its original intentions, we can't jump on bandwagons for the sake of money or public relations.

Running Waterlution has been good for me on so many personal and professional levels. I've never felt more inspired, more connected, more alive and purposeful. And finding balance within my life has given me the confidence that I'll be on this extraordinary journey for a very long time. There's a great need for what Waterlution does, and I plan to be there every step of the way.

■ ■ ■ ■ ■

KAREN KUN is the director of Waterlution (www.waterlution.org) and publisher of *Corporate Knights* magazine (www.corporateknights.ca). She has two films in development on Canadian and global water issues with her creative partner in Edmonton and another film in production in Toronto that tells the story of the rise of a local municipal councillor. She lives in Toronto.

D. Simon Jackson

T
HE GREATEST GIFT my parents ever gave me was the gift of travel. We didn't visit the exotic wonders of the world or the sunny beaches of Hawaii, but for several years when I was very young, we would pack up our car and drive—across Canada, to Alaska, through the American Southwest. On one such trip when I was seven, our final stop was Yellowstone National Park, an untouched wilderness in northwestern Wyoming. It was there that I saw my first wild bear—a mother grizzly with two cubs—in a meadow almost a mile from the road. Seeing those bears captured my imagination and sparked my curiosity. A passion was born.

Then one night, as I watched the evening news with my family, I saw a story about the Kodiak bear in Alaska and the planned developments—logging, new roads, a resort—that threatened its habitat. When I heard the news, my brewing interest for bears boiled over, and I was determined to help. My parents were hardly activists, but when I asked them what I could do, they suggested writing letters or raising money, so I decided to do both. Like every other seven-year-old I set up a lemonade stand, and through the summer months I sold lemonade to raise money for the Kodiak bear. I raised sixty dollars and wrote letters to then–Prime Minister Brian Mulroney and then-President George Bush Sr.

Two months later I received a letter in the mail announcing that the Kodiak bear's habitat was protected—the bears were saved. To my mind, it was my sixty dollars and two letters that saved them. Although that clearly wasn't the case, it was true that every person who cared about the issue contributed to a collective effort that saved the Kodiak bear. That realization was the most important lesson I ever learned: that one person—regardless of age or where he or she lived—could make a difference for all life. This knowledge has been a powerful tool that allowed me to overcome the many roadblocks I would soon face in my quest to save another bear—a rare white bear that lives only in my home province of British Columbia—in a campaign that's come to define the majority of my youth.

The spirit bear, also known as the white Kermode, is a genetically unique subspecies of the black bear that lives in the temperate rainforest of B.C.'s north central coast. Over the past hundred years, settlements and resource extraction gradually robbed this bear of a large portion of its home, leaving it with one last ecosystem. The spirit bear's future hinged on saving this piece of land.

I knew I had to help. I began by challenging the students at my school to write letters. At first I was shy and I hated public speaking, but I knew I had to get over my fear if I was going to be an effective force on behalf of the bears. Ultimately

I achieved some success: I was able to capture the imagination of enough students that I collected seven hundred letters of support and mailed them to Glen Clark, British Columbia's premier at the time. A few months later I received the premier's reply. Disappointingly, it made no promises and offered no hope that his government would save the spirit bear. I was shocked. Thinking back to my lemonade stand and how my sixty dollars and two letters helped save the Kodiak bear, I wondered how seven hundred letters couldn't save the spirit bear. I realized that although the letters had made the government aware of the issue, I would need to take further action to gain widespread support.

I began by writing letters to the editors of local papers and challenging other schools to get involved. But I knew that to engage more people I would need to become an expert. To learn more about the public policy aspect of this issue I contacted every organization, business, government agency, educational institution, and individual named in published articles about the bear. I wanted to understand the issue from both sides to present a balanced case as to why this bear needed to be protected—I wanted to stress that there were no "bad guys" in this campaign and that everyone, on all sides of the issue, could embrace the protection of the region.

As support started to grow, so too did the number of young people who wanted to do more than write letters. At every school talk I gave I found that young people wanted to belong to something—anything—that would respect their role in the campaign and offer a loud, distinct voice in the fight to save the spirit bear. So one afternoon, over my mother's hamburgers and chocolate cake, I asked a few friends for their help in creating an organization, a group we named the Spirit Bear Youth Coalition. Aside from ensuring young people had a voice in this issue, one of our top priorities was to engage the unengaged—to show people who normally wouldn't support an environmental cause why they could support this one.

Starting an organization was easier said than done. We built it slowly—starting with young people from the North Shore of Vancouver where I grew up and expanding outwards, signing people up at every event in which we participated. In fact, on many occasions we weren't invited; we simply showed up when we thought the audience might be interested in our message. We would hand out information sheets and attempt to collect as many names and addresses as possible. But although we were growing, I knew we needed a more powerful voice to help us spread our message and catch the media's attention.

Every day I would get up at 6:00 AM to read the papers and listen to the radio to see if anything was happening that day in Vancouver that could help my efforts. One day I heard on the radio that Prince William was going to be in Vancouver, and I knew immediately that we had to gain his support. I bussed down to one of his public appearances only to find hundreds of screaming teenage girls waving roses and asking the prince to marry them. I made my way though the crowd, brandishing a book about the spirit bear and shouting to gain their attention. A sudden silence took hold of the screaming girls; people were shocked to see a guy, let alone a guy yelling about bears. That pause was all I needed—it gave me the chance to talk to Prince William. He was interested in what I told him and offered me his support ... in front of the media.

The best part of that event was seeing the premier pacing a few metres away, fretting about our conversation. But I also learned two powerful lessons that spring day. First, I was a fifteen-year-old kid with no power, no influence, and no connections—yet I was able to speak with one of the best-known people in the world. I realized if I could reach the prince, I could reach anyone. Second, I'd initially wondered if the prince would actually care about a bear that lived only in B.C., but it quickly occurred to me that although the panda lives only in China, we all care about its future. The spirit bear may live only in British Columbia, but it's Canada's panda—a global treasure whose place on the planet every person the world over could and should care about safeguarding.

I believe that the key to success in every campaign is 99 per cent hard work and 1 per cent good luck. My efforts ran into roadblocks every step of the way. Teachers didn't want their students getting engaged in politics. My parents were nervous about how this campaign would affect my studies. I lost my friends, not because they didn't support me, but because saving a bear was *different*, and in high school different isn't always cool. It was hell—I was bullied every day from the moment I walked into my school; I even had to eat lunch by myself in the washroom to avoid the name calling. And when I got home, I had to deal with the politics of saving the spirit bear.

Anyone—especially a teenage kid—trying to change public policy in British Columbia on an issue affecting the forest industry in the 1990s faced an uphill battle. We weren't antilogging, and we weren't out to put people out of a job—in fact, our campaign message was built on balance. We wanted to protect the minimum area of land needed to protect the bear's gene pool while addressing the local economic concerns associated with conservation. We believed that logging elsewhere, coupled with investment into economic diversification ventures in conservation-based industries, would create a vibrant economy that would far surpass any planned logging in the spirit bear's habitat. Yet in a province known for its vicious politics, thoughtful debate was sidelined by rhetoric-filled

sound bites. Young people's views were dismissed as irrel-
evant. Our message was met by skeptics and the occasional
threat, making a tough campaign even tougher.

Every morning when my alarm would go off and it was rain-
ing outside, I would ask myself, "Why do I want to get out of
bed today? Why do I want to go to school and be bullied? Why
would I want to tackle the ugly politics of this issue and face
the skeptical majority?" And then I'd remember: five hundred
kilometres north of my home was a bear whose future was
uncertain. I was not the smartest or even the best-equipped
person to help save this bear, but I was likely one of its most
passionate champions. By giving up, I would be giving up on
this bear, and I would have to be prepared to grow up in a world
where the spirit bear might no longer exist. That kind of future
wasn't something I was willing to accept. So I kept going.

Finally, our 1 per cent of good luck came knocking at my
door, when *Time* magazine selected me as one of their sixty
Heroes for the Planet. I was one of only six young people
from around the world to receive this honour. I don't consider
myself a hero, and to this day I don't know how they found
out about our campaign. But the benefits of their recognition went way beyond having my picture published. It gave
the Youth Coalition credibility, it proved young people could
make a difference, and it gave us a remarkable platform to talk
about the bears.

Shortly after the *Time* article appeared, the fight to save the
spirit bear went from a high-school letter-writing campaign to
become a broad-based global issue, helping to bring forestry
companies, local and provincial government agencies, First
Nations representatives, environmental groups, and the tour-
ism industry to the negotiating table. This dialogue paved the
way for a historic land-use agreement in 2001 that protected
half of the spirit bear's last intact habitat and deferred logging

in the other half. The agreement went on to create a framework for conservation on the entire B.C. coast, which, when it was ratified by the B.C. government on April 4 of that year, was labelled around the world as historic and precedent-setting.

On February 7, 2006, almost five years later, the B.C. government made another land-use decision that continued to work towards a sustainable vision for the B.C. coast and the protection of the spirit bear. But although two-thirds of this bear's habitat is now legally set aside, a third remains more endangered today than ever before. Despite all our campaign's successes, unless we protect that final third—an area known as the Green watershed—we won't be able to save the spirit bear. Some may say, "With so much land set aside, why push for more?" Well, even though the bear's core habitat has been saved, the watersheds that surround the area haven't been safeguarded. If we do not protect the Green, we run the risk of what's called a swamping effect: the logging in the watershed would force black bears that don't carry the spirit bear's unique gene to migrate en masse into the last stable population of bears that do carry the gene, diluting the gene pool and over time causing the spirit bear to disappear.

Simply put, protecting the watershed has always been our ecological bottom line. Saving the spirit bear means saving the Green watershed. Yet with more support for this endeavour than any other conservation issue in Canadian history, according to a Statistics Canada study in 2001, we know we'll save the Green, proving to every skeptical young person who lent this bear their voice that they did make a difference. We will be able to say with confidence that our spirit bear will forever be wild and free.

Today our network spans more than sixty countries and numbers more than six million, all working to protect the spirit bear's last intact habitat. We've reunited the team responsible for *Lion King* to help us produce *The Spirit Bear*, Hollywood's first major animated movie that will also help protect its namesake. The movie is scheduled for release in the spring of 2008, and a portion of every ticket sold will go towards saving the spirit bear. We hope the profits from the movie will allow us to invest in the economic potential of isolated coastal communities that border the spirit bear's habitat, creating jobs in new sectors and showing that saving the spirit bear can be accomplished without disregarding economic, environmental, and social concerns.

For years, when I spoke at schools about the spirit bear, students would approach me and say, "Simon, I'm only one person, and if I don't bother to write a letter then it won't make a difference." And to that I would answer, "You're right. If you don't make your voice heard, then you won't make a difference. No one will know what you think. But if every person said, 'Yes, I can make a difference. I will do my part; I will make my voice heard!' then think of the possibilities." Twenty-five thousand letters made their way into the premier's office in the months leading up to the first land-use agreement in 2001. I know it was one of those letters that the premier picked up and that promted him to say, "What are we going to do about the spirit bear?" It was one person who put the issue over the top, but it took all 24,999 letters to make that one letter count.

The story of my journey from selling lemonade to helping produce a Hollywood movie may seem, well, sensational enough for a Hollywood movie. But there was nothing unique about my experiences. Anybody could have done what I've been doing for any issue they believe in—whether it's trying to protect a peregrine falcon's nest in their neighbourhood or trying to rid the world of cancer, there are no insignificant endeavours. Every time someone stands up to act to improve the lot of others, they are helping to create a better world. I was driven by my passion and the good fortune of knowing, thanks to my luck with the lemonade stand at the age of seven, that I could succeed. We each have the power to create change, and we're even stronger when we work together, united as one voice. I call this the power of one.

■ ■ ■ ■ ■

SIMON JACKSON founded the Spirit Bear Youth Coalition (www. spiritbearyouth.org) at the age of thirteen. He recently co-founded

 Helade Productions to produce *The Spirit Bear* (www.spiritbearmovie.com), slated for worldwide release in 2008. His life inspired a TV movie, *Spirit Bear: The Simon Jackson Story.* He remains the full-time volunteer chairman of the Spirit Bear Youth Coalition, in addition to his roles as executive producer of *The Spirit Bear,* principal of Jackson Strategies, and member of several boards and advisory committees.

Lyndsay Poaps

P EOPLE ASK ME all the time if I miss politics. No, I say, how could I? Politics is what I do every day, whether it's as an elected official or a community organizer.

For a long time I've described myself as a community youth developer, which is a fancy way of saying youth activist. In 1999 I was coordinating events for the Sierra Club of Canada when I suddenly shifted my focus to fighting the Multilateral Agreement on Investment (MAI), an international trade agreement that twenty-nine governments—including Canada's—were negotiating without public consultation. The MAI proposed a set of universal investment laws that would give corporations powers that superseded national laws and human rights, putting the interests of regular citizens in jeopardy.

As I became more involved in the anti-MAI campaign, though, I discovered another disturbing parallel with my earlier activism: none of the planning process, events, or educational materials were youth friendly. Young people were relegated to volunteer positions where they spent most of their time stuffing envelopes. In response, ten other young people and I decided to put together a conference on the MAI for youth. The conference was the brainchild of Kevin Millsip, a fellow activist who shared my concern about the MAI and who was also disillusioned with organizations that didn't know how to work with young people. While we were organizing the conference, the MAI negotiations collapsed, so we shifted the conference's focus to broader issues of globalization.

The response was overwhelming. Youth from all across the country came to Vancouver to participate. We turned the traditional conference structure on its head. Young people facilitated the entire event and led a number of the interactive workshops. Throughout the three-day event, people kept coming up to us and telling us we had to find a way to keep it going.

Kevin and I shared great collaborative synergy, and with the support of the other organizers, we channelled the energy and excitement the conference generated into founding Check Your Head (CYH), an organization to engage and educate youth about global issues through critical thinking and popular education.

We started by delivering workshops throughout Vancouver and the Lower Mainland. Our interactive style and timely topics—quizzes and role-playing games to discuss current affairs such as the World Trade Organization protests in Seattle— | 59
made us popular with students and teachers.

At CYH we respected the knowledge and skills of young people and spent a lot of time making sure we validated them. Meanwhile, CYH started to play a role in Vancouver's growing youth community. Throughout the late 1990s and into early 2001, Vancouver city council wasn't responding to our needs. From issues as specific as skateboarding to processes as broad as urban planning, young people were left out or involved only as tokens. It almost felt like it was illegal to be young in this city.

During this time CYH collaborated with the Canadian Federation of Students, the Environmental Youth Alliance, the B.C. Teachers' Federation, YouthCO AIDS Society, and other organizations on different initiatives that provided engagement opportunities for young people. These collaborations led to strong networks between youth-driven and youth-serving organizations across a spectrum of sectors, from groups focused on homelessness to environmental activists. We demanded that people of our generation have a meaningful say in how the city was run.

Out of these networks a group called Youth Driven took shape to help increase the capacity of youth-driven agencies so that they could run more efficiently and reach more people. Through Youth Driven the youth community conducted its own needs assessment and created a document outlining the needs of Vancouver's young people and a plan for the city to meet those needs. Every year Youth Driven held a conference to introduce young people to the city's many youth organizations and to showcase and celebrate their work and initiatives. Youth Driven met regularly, and it was important for Check Your Head to participate, because the nature of CYH's globally focused work meant we often collaborated with adult organizations. Youth Driven provided a forum for CYH and other groups to discuss the mutual challenges they faced, and it was the most collaborative, encouraging, dynamic environment I've ever known. This community work was challenging and fun, and it provided me with abilities and experiences that have helped me ever since.

In 1999 the Coalition of Progressive Electors (COPE) approached Kevin Millsip and me to work with them on their municipal election campaign. I was extremely skeptical of COPE, the party system, and the idea that voting could make a real difference. I thought the municipal electoral system was flawed—undemocratic even—and that the same old white people always got elected. I was convinced that only people with giant egos and their own self-interest at heart ran for public office.

The campaign was frantic and nothing like I expected. Most members of the COPE staff were under forty. They sought legitimacy and were serious about winning, but they also wanted us to have fun and follow our instincts. They had a wide range of interests and wanted to accomplish everything from adding cycling lanes to ending the dumping of the city's raw sewage into the ocean. I got a real education working on this campaign. I started to understand all the ways the local government affected my life, but I also saw that it didn't always reflect my generation's needs or interests. The campaign opened my eyes to how political parties actually worked, and I saw what they were able to do that non-profit organizations simply couldn't. A political party can spend as much money as it wants on advertising for its point of view and doesn't need to be seen as unbiased—its whole reason for being is to be partisan. One aspect of the campaign didn't surprise me, though: nearly all the candidates were middle-aged or older.

COPE didn't elect as many candidates as it had hoped. Even so, the staff were committed to increasing party membership, maintaining a voice in municipal issues, and building energy for the next election. COPE invited me to sit on the party's executive, where I served as youth representative for the next three years. My involvement with COPE was the perfect complement to my work with Check Your Head: one focused on local issues, the other on international ones.

By the time I was encouraged to run for the park board in 2002, I felt that my years of being a youth advocate had fostered a desire in me to be closer to the levers of change. Local politics seemed like an obvious venue and the right place to devote my energy. The global justice movement had become a movement of travelling activists, and I was more interested in trying to effect change and putting my beliefs into practice here at home. Bigger-picture activism had started to make me feel powerless, and meanwhile I had learned how much of an impact municipal governments have on people's lives every day. Vancouver is known as young and vibrant, yet those qualities weren't reflected in the faces of the people who ran the city. I wanted to fix this deficiency.

COPE members and the youth community supported me. While I was running for park board I was able to get important issues into the media. It was a perfect platform to talk about how young people were excluded from creating and programming their own recreational opportunities at the city's community centres and to bring issues of ethical purchasing and climate change to the municipal level. At the beginning of the campaign, a long-time COPE member congratulated me on running and said, "That's great—you'll be great. You won't win, of course, but you'll be great." That comment calmed me down through the campaign; in that frame of mind I was able to campaign honestly and without being paralyzed by the desire to be elected.

COPE won the 2002 municipal and mayoral elections. A lot of factors contributed to the victory: the opposition was fractured, our candidate for mayor was well-liked—and the inspiration for a popular CBC TV show, *Da Vinci's Inquest*—and the citizens of Vancouver wanted a change. I was shocked when I found out I won, and the hundreds of people surrounding me on election night were all jubilant and stunned. I felt exhilarated and scared, but mostly happy for the people who'd worked so hard for so many years to bring a progressive majority to city hall.

The following three years were hard and exciting. I learned so much about government and human nature. Many of us who were elected were rookies; people who already worked for the city were afraid of the changes we'd make, and the city's elites were set on not giving us a chance. Internal disputes within COPE compounded our troubles.

Meanwhile, I struggled with being outside my protective, youth-friendly bubble. Not everyone was receptive to me—at twenty-three, I was the youngest-ever elected official in the city of Vancouver. I often got double-takes and sideways glances. At a community meeting to discuss fixing up a park held at one of the organizers' homes, I sat down among the chatting neighbours before the meeting began. After ten minutes someone asked why we hadn't started the meeting. The woman next to me answered that we couldn't start until the "park board lady" got there. I said, "I am the 'park board lady.'" The woman's face flushed scarlet with embarrassment, but not before she squeezed out, "Sorry, but you're so young!" I had to work extra hard that first year to prove I was a legitimate park board commissioner, not just a kid interested only in youth issues.

That said, I was able to do something for young people, and these moments made me feel that joining the "institution" was worth the effort and sacrifice. In September 2005 a new skate park called the Plaza was opened in Vancouver. It's the biggest street-style skate park of its kind in North America and had taken seven years of struggle to convince the city to approve and build it. When I got elected I made it a priority to ensure the plans were completed. I was returning home from the opening ceremony when I ran into a couple of guys who'd lobbied hard for the park through an organization they had founded called the Vancouver Skate Park Coalition. They showed such commitment and dedication, coming back year after year to try to make this park a reality. One of them, Travis Cutler, skated up to the very edge of the park, flipped up his skateboard, and said, "Hey, Lyndsay, thanks for making it worth voting!"

Unfortunately, my disillusion with COPE grew: I found that the party sometimes squandered opportunities and that its policies didn't always match its politics. COPE had always characterized itself as open to debate and dialogue, but over the three years of our term communication broke down, and many of the elected members of our party stopped talking to each other. Infighting and the absence of cohesion among the elected members of COPE allowed the opposition to exploit a division within the party, and they successfully defeated proposed reforms to the city's electoral system that had been a fundamental component of COPE's platform since it was created thirty years ago. Yet, even as I grew frustrated with the party, I was becoming ever more impressed by the people in the city who were working hard to build their communities. The volunteers who help run community centres, the people who organize street parties, the members of community gardens—these citizens were the people I connected to.

Ultimately, a political split on city council divided COPE, and some of its members left to form their own party. By this time most of the young people involved with COPE had left—

they had either been alienated or pushed out. Politics wasn't the problem—for the most part people agreed on our mandate and philosophy. But council members had limited experience working in team settings. Most of them were used to having the last word when making decisions, which got in the way of reaching compromises. Each side would try to drag the rest of the elected COPE members into the dispute and force us to take sides. I realized that working with people whose politics I shared but whose attitudes I found disrespectful just wasn't for me.

Being involved in a political party and getting elected was like having two full-time jobs. At the end of three years I didn't have the energy to pursue them both anymore. I always wanted my work to make the best use of my time, but COPE had started to feel like a drain on my enthusiasm for anything political. I didn't want to become one of those politicians whose only motivation was to get re-elected. So in 2005, instead of running again, I went back to school.

I now sit on the board of my local community centre, and I selectively get involved in different community initiatives. I have a sense of the amazing things this city is capable of when it's working for the interests of present and future citizens. And when I returned to community activism, where I could focus on my own priorities and on my communities' needs rather than having to balance those of all of Vancouver, I was reminded of why I ran for office in the first place. Stepping away has allowed me to renew the passion in my love affair with this city.

I'm grateful that the role of elected politician has been demystified for me. Before I was elected, I always thought politicians possessed some expertise that eluded me. But I've discovered that the best type of politician is one who has passion for his or her community, understands how that community is part of a whole, and enjoys working with a variety of people. I may have had some negative experiences on the park board, but now I know I can do it. And I know that electoral politics will be there for me just as soon as I'm ready to jump back in.

■ ■ ■ ■ ■

IN 2002 LYNDSAY POAPS became the youngest elected official in Vancouver's history, serving as a city park board commissioner from 2002 to 2005. Before her election Lyndsay co-founded Check Your Head (www.checkyourhead.org), an organization that encourages youth to think about global and local issues. She is an Action Canada fellow, a board member of the Think City Society, and a board mem-

ber with the Trout Lake Community Centre. She is currently working on a Master of Public Policy degree at Simon Fraser University. In her spare time she is developing the Vancouver Public Spaces Network and teaching herself the melodica.

Richard Hoshino

■ ■ ■

BUTTERING BREAD, SERVING hot food on paper plates, passing out ketchup, and wiping up tables—would you believe this work was the highlight of my week?

I volunteered at a Sunday Suppers program for the underprivileged in Halifax. Close to three hundred people walked through the doors of St. Andrew's Church every Sunday afternoon where a caring team of volunteers treated them to a warm meal and unlimited coffee and juice. We served people in our community who were down on their luck, from single mothers struggling below the poverty line to older men with disabilities who couldn't find a steady job. We learned that our friends from Sunday Suppers weren't so-called welfare bums—a horrible term—but real people looking for hope, and somehow they found a little bit each week.

And yet, until a few years ago, such simple acts of service

had no place on my to-do list. For a long time, I couldn't care less about volunteering.

I've lived a life of incredible privilege. My parents came to Toronto from Japan just before I was born, and like many immigrants, they made sacrifices for their child. They worked hard to send me to private school and provide me with unlimited opportunities. They instilled in me a love of learning I've never lost and taught me the value of ambition and hard work.

They also recognized my aptitude for mathematics. In my last year of high school I represented Canada at the International Mathematical Olympiad; later I studied math on a scholarship at the University of Waterloo and continued my education as a graduate student at Dalhousie University in Halifax. Outside the classroom I fostered intercultural dialogue among youth, gave presentations on innovative mathematics pedagogy at a number of conferences, and established successful math outreach programs for high school students and their teachers. Although all of these efforts were important and appeared altruistic, I was solely focused on my self-serving ambitions. I freely admit that I piled up responsibilities to make my résumé stand out and that all of my initiatives were to advance my career.

In 2003 I received a fellowship with Action Canada, a program to identify and develop future Canadian leaders. I relished this unique opportunity to be exposed to important public policy issues, and I looked forward to networking with some of Canada's most influential young people. I considered "leadership" strictly a matter of power and influence and hoped my Action Canada experience would increase my stature.

I didn't at all expect a complete paradigm shift—the realization that leadership isn't about power or influence but about *service*. One experience in particular had a transformative effect on my life.

In September 2003 the twenty Action Canada fellows met in Vancouver for a one-week conference. We spent a full day examining the issues facing Vancouver's Downtown Eastside. We toured the infamous neighbourhood, seeing for ourselves the drug use, prostitution, and extraordinary poverty that plagued its streets. That evening we watched an award-winning documentary by Nellie Wild called FIX: *The Story of An Addicted City*. The film followed the lives of Ann Livingston and Dean Wilson, two of the major lobbyists for a controversial safe injection site in the Downtown Eastside, the first such facility in Canada. Dean is a former IBM salesman who has been addicted to heroin for almost thirty-five years. His partner, Ann, had never used drugs in her life and had recently converted to Christianity.

One scene spoke deeply to me. Ann is sitting by herself in a church, quietly praying during the service. No one is seated within five feet of her because of her ties to the heroin community. Despite the Biblical commands to love and care for one another, no one approaches Ann to engage in conversation or offer their support or prayers. Ann speaks directly into the camera in response to the hypocrisy around her: "There really is only one message that Christ had, and it was that you're to always reach out to people who have nothing. You're always to stand in the most uncomfortable place with the ugly, the rejected, the smelly, the sick. Whatever it is for you. And be in that place where you're going, 'I hate this'—and doing it anyway."

These words transformed me. As a Christian myself, I reflected on what I was doing to reach out to the underprivileged. The answer was obvious: I was doing absolutely nothing. Ann quoted the Parable of the Sheep and the Goats (Matthew 25:31–46), a lesson I knew in my head but not in my heart. This parable teaches Christians to serve those who have been rejected by society, by feeding the hungry, comforting the sick, and providing clothes to those in need. I had convinced myself that my hectic work weeks excused me from helping others. I felt strongly that each hour spent volunteering would be an hour lost doing something more important. As I watched the documentary that night, I recognized my self-righteous hypocrisy and discovered that through Ann's words God was speaking directly to me.

After the screening we were invited to dinner with the people involved in the film. Ann and Dean were both there and had brought along their ten-month-old baby, Joseph, whom I asked if I could hold. I can't describe the thoughts that rushed through my mind as I held this beautiful baby, knowing his father was a heroin addict who didn't have a community to support him with compassion and love. As Ann said in the documentary, Christians like me were doing nothing for the Dean Wilsons of our society. As I clutched Joseph in my arms, I heard a voice from deep within my heart: "Richard, what are you doing to help my people?"

As soon as I got home I began volunteering at The Fish, a coffee house ministry for the underprivileged in Halifax, held every Saturday night. I met people I never cared to associate myself with before, like those with severe physical disabilities and others suffering from drug and alcohol addictions. I had unfairly assumed that because they had not achieved successful careers that they would have nothing to teach me. Working with these individuals was a new and difficult experience: I was a rich private-school kid who knew virtually no one who'd come from difficult circumstances. I felt self-conscious and awkward, and it was hard to make conversation.

But slowly I built trust with those I served, playing cards and cribbage with them and showing them a mathematical strategy to play Connect Four—my graduate degrees finally coming in handy! As I got to know my new friends and heard their stories, my presumptions dissolved. I befriended, among many others, a woman who acquired HIV through a bad blood transfusion, and a remarkable blind man who wrote for a street newspaper to raise awareness of poverty issues and who sat on the executive committee of the North American Street Newspaper Association.

I discovered, to my surprise, that many of Halifax's welfare recipients either worked or were upgrading their skills to return to the workforce. Often because of various mental or physical challenges, welfare recipients mostly worked menial jobs like cleaning floors or washing dishes at a restaurant. After the 70 per cent clawback they had to give the provincial government for working while on social assistance, welfare recipients earned less than two dollars an hour for their labour. Despite this challenge, many pressed on with the determination that they could climb out of poverty and secure a better future for themselves and their children. The Fish was a remarkable place because it didn't elevate the volunteers above those they served; instead, it provided a space of genuine interaction among equals, and I learned so much just by watching and listening to this interaction.

My new friends challenged me to think more holistically about the community I lived in and to find proactive ways to serve it. My high school mandated that each student complete a set number of community service hours each year. To complete my hours I deliberately selected easy tasks that required minimal effort and no commitment. Looking back, I can see that my volunteerism was a patronizing form of charity that meant nothing to me. I used to focus on what I would get from volunteering. Now, I focus strictly on the people I serve, and I aim to meet their needs to the best of my ability. Once I finally understood and took seriously my commitment to service I found myself empowered and becoming more compassionate, less judgmental, and more cognizant of how I spent my time and money. I discovered that the more I learned to willingly serve others, the easier it was to share God's love with those less fortunate.

When I learned about the Sunday Suppers program, I started volunteering there, too, finding it even more rewarding than The Fish. I only volunteered for four hours each week, but still I feel that what I did made a small yet tangible difference in my community, which grew to include more than just other mathematicians. Two friends from The Fish once pooled their leftover savings from their monthly disability assistance and treated me to a magnificent Chinese buffet. We spoke for nearly five hours and gained about ten pounds each. I was so challenged and inspired by the compassion and generosity of our guests at The Fish and Sunday Suppers.

Unless I was out of town I never missed either of my volunteer commitments, regardless of how busy I was with work. It shouldn't have been a surprise to me, but the more I volunteered, the happier I became.

After graduate school I moved to Ottawa to work for the federal government. Here I've found a remarkable organization called The Mission. It has an emergency shelter for over two hundred guests a night, chaplaincy services, a hospice, programs for addiction recovery and job training, and a state-of-the-art kitchen that served over 333,000 meals in 2004. Currently I volunteer in the kitchen, but my great hope is to be involved in The Mission's "Discovery University" program, where local professors provide free post-secondary education to people living below the poverty line.

Similar "free university" initiatives in Vancouver, Calgary, and Halifax already play a vital role in those communities. Such programs go beyond basic needs and "job skills" to provide underprivileged people with an opportunity to engage in subjects such as philosophy, sociology, anthropology, and English literature. Many students develop a new thirst for acquiring knowledge and improve their abilities to resolve conflicts and solve problems. Graduates of the program have gone on to become more active in their communities, take up volunteerism, become self-employed, and in some cases, enrol in full-time studies at a college or university.

Volunteerism, I've discovered, isn't about logging hours or having something altruistic to add to a résumé. It's about serving others from a willing and cheerful heart. I'm so thankful to have learned this lesson, and through my genuine desire to serve others, I feel I now have a closer relationship with my God.

RICHARD HOSHINO is originally from Toronto but proudly calls himself a Maritimer after having spent four wonderful years in Atlantic Canada. Richard currently works as a Senior Project Officer for the Canada Border Services Agency (CBSA), hired under the federal government's prestigious Recruitment of Policy Leaders initiative. At CBSA, Richard uses mathematics to help improve the security and efficiency of the Canadian border. He continues to volunteer for The Mission in Ottawa (www.ottawamission. com).

MODERN INUK
ON THE MOVE

Miali-Elise Coley

WHEN NUNAVUT WAS created as an official territory with its own government in 1999, there were a lot of expectations for positive change: more job opportunities for Inuit, fewer social problems, and lower suicide rates. Yet although there have been a number of benefits, many problems were also born with this new territory. The lack of trained local workers meant an influx of Southerners. The population of our capital, Iqaluit, increased dramatically in just a few years, a surge that brought with it a number of social challenges. Newcomers introduced new street drugs into our community and put further pressure on our resources.

It's extremely difficult to deal with the aftermath of colonialism. Here in Nunavut, people have been taught a very limited version of our history, and our traditional culture is fragile.

Since I was young I've tried to adapt to the changes and serve as a positive influence by participating in peer counselling and anti-drug campaigns and encouraging friends to speak Inuktitut. Living in the North, I am completely isolated from other ethnic groups, including other indigenous peoples. Thankfully I've had opportunities to travel and to gain insight into other cultures and their similar struggles. I've seen that there's still a lot of pain from the legacy of colonization even hundreds of years later. What I seek to understand is how, in our own journey as Inuit, we can take steps to avoid years of further suffering and to begin our healing today.

My family, coming from two completely different places— the North and Jamaica—has had a big impact on my activism. My mother has ensured that my three brothers and I are aware of our own roots. She's a true inspiration who has always exuded a strength I admire. She raised us all on her own (though she's now married). She taught us never to limit ourselves and to explore all possibilities. She often says, "I can't offer you everything in my culture because I have lost a lot, but what I have I can pass on to you." I really value the knowledge and wisdom she has given us.

I was brought up to speak Inuktitut, eat traditional food, observe people who make traditional clothing, and respect elders. I practise the ancient art of throat singing. I go camping with my family, where elders teach us how to use all the parts of the animal. When my two younger brothers bring back caribou from hunting, we prepare various foods out of the catch, like *nikku*, caribou jerky. Inuit hunters always share the food they catch—it's a big part of our culture to give thanks through sharing.

My father's Jamaican perspective has also been very important to me. I've been able to draw strength and inspiration from two beautiful worlds. I have my family that raised me in the North and my father and his family, who have always been involved in my life.

In the fall of 2004 I spent two months in Jamaica with my grandmother. It was the first time I had actually lived there and learned about the life of my father's side of the family—it was an incredible experience. Having grown up in Iqaluit, speaking Inuktitut at home with my Inuk mother, I wanted to know a lot more about my identity as a person of Jamaican descent.

During my first week people would ask me if I was melting, and they peppered me with all sorts of questions about "Eskimos." One woman came to my grandmother's veranda and asked me where I slept: she thought a regular room would be too hot for me. I told her my grandmother had cleaned out the fridge and that I was sleeping in there. She said, "Me understand!" though I don't think she got the joke. And why should she have? A lot of people, in Jamaica and even in Canada, simply don't know anything about "Eskimos"; they still imagine fur-clad people carrying harpoons.

It's exciting to teach people who wouldn't otherwise know what life is like up in the North. Across Canada, for example, I've noticed a prejudice against Inuit for being raw-meat eaters. I'm quick to defend the subsistence lifestyle and justify its benefits. Aside from the fact that historically, raw meat was virtually all we had, food from the land is also extremely nutritious—it really is all we've needed for a rich, balanced diet. We don't want to switch to alternatives, and not just because they're more expensive and less healthy. Hunting and eating our catch is the Inuit's natural way of life—even a form of therapy. It's how we provide for our families and the people in our communities. (Ask any dietician: it's nothing like eating raw chicken or raw beef.)

Now, however, our generation fears that our food is contaminated and that it's not providing the same nourishment it used to, in part because of the pollution of our land and in part because of the effects of climate change. Scientists have reported increasing mercury levels in the fatty parts of northern animals, and experienced hunters have died falling through what is now unpredictable ice. It's overwhelming to imagine that one day Inuit might be afraid to eat country food. It would mean such a disconnection from our culture and our longstanding relationship with nature.

When I was fifteen I worked for a birthright land claims organization called Qikiqtani Inuit Association. It represents Inuit communities in the Baffin region and works towards protecting and promoting Inuit rights and values. I started off working with an after-school program for underprivileged children that offered a safe and structured environment for fun and learning. The program met a need in the community for constructive indoor and outdoor activities for kids to have fun and learn about health and nutrition.

The following summer Qajaaq Ellsworth, the regional youth coordinator of Qikiqtani Inuit Association, and I developed a proposal to run a full-out summer camp for the children to further promote healthy living. Getting community support took a lot of work, but I was up to the task. I'm happy to report that nine years later, the Sprouts program continues to run each summer. Kids are really excited about Sprouts and ask me about it year-round.

Since then I've become active in other ways, from chairing the Inuit Circumpolar Youth Council to dealing with climate change issues through several different organizations. As a youth leader I have spoken to various audiences about how global warming, by threatening our traditional hunting lifestyle, is affecting young Inuit. In 2004 I travelled to Winnipeg and many cities in Ontario on the "Communities and the Impact of Climate Change" speakers' tour sponsored by CUSO, an NGO that supports social justice and environmental activism. More recently I've become interested in education. I've come to feel very strongly about preserving and promoting our rich culture and history by passing on our knowledge to the next generation. With all of the changes the Inuit are experiencing, I think we need to hold fast to our values and focus on our strengths and our identity.

We need to start listening more to our elders. We're always seeking knowledge outside of our communities, but many of the answers are right here at home. I feel like we're just waiting to be completely assimilated when we could be using the resources we already have, and drawing strength from who we are as a people, to determine our own destiny.

When I was in high school I had a hard time learning about European history, because my heart wanted to learn Inuit history and our traditional ways. To pursue this knowledge I enrolled myself in an accredited college program for Inuit in Ottawa called Nunavut Sivuniksavut, or "our land, our future," where I gained a strong footing in our political history, studied land claims, and learned about our ancient cultural arts.

This program really influenced my thinking and allowed me to understand our unique story as Inuit: I learned about the arrival of the first whalers and missionaries and how school teachers mistreated Inuit children in the residential school era. I still can't believe we didn't study any of this history in high school, where our curriculum is adopted from the Alberta education system. I'm becoming more fervent about getting involved in education and curriculum development for Nunavut.

Currently I'm working on an Inuit language "hipification" strategy with the Inuit Circumpolar Youth Council. We coined the term after we determined there was a need to popularize the Inuit language. Our campaign aims to produce a report that will be available to schools, commissioners, and language stakeholders to give them an Inuit youth perspective on the importance of preserving our language. Sometimes we forget just how vital language is to the success and health of a people. It's at the core of our lives.

Language defines us in a way that's hard for English speakers in the South to understand. For example, although I'm half Jamaican, my "Inukness" has never been an issue for other Inuit, as far as I can tell. I speak Inuktitut, and I have the personality and the mentality of an Inuk. It's only when I became more involved in activism as a teenager that my appearance sometimes surprised people. It's almost as though they had to shake off the fact that I look black. But it was almost always with Southerners that I had this problem and that I realized the colour of my skin was even an issue.

I've come to fully accept my identity as a Jamaican Inuk. When most Inuit meet me, they compliment me on my appearance and even say they'd like to have mixed children of their own. In fact, people have wanted to adopt my children for as long as I can remember. This idea of black and Inuit is unique, and it's something people seem to want—the opposite of what a lot of people would expect.

I want to take my grounding in the North and use it to contribute positively to the expansion and growth of Nunavut, especially by developing materials for the education we need. There are many stories, like those of my grandparents, that are incredibly interesting; with today's technology we have new ways of presenting these stories to a younger audience. Inuit and non-Inuit teachers in Nunavut don't have the resources they need to teach effectively about our culture and history, and I want to be one of the teachers who help create effective and valuable teaching tools for Nunavut's new education system.

There are many active, positive-minded young people who also want to work for the betterment of our territory. Despite the social issues and hardships, I have made it a personal commitment not to complain about our current situation. We are in a hard but wonderful place. We are the rightful owners of this land and have the capacity to take care of it as we have for thousands of years. As a Jamaican Inuk I will do everything I can to continue to contribute towards a better place for all Northerners. I want to be a voice and a catalyst for positive change.

■ ■ ■ ■ ■

MIALI-ELISE COLEY is a youth advocate for the North. As youth coordinator for the Qikiqtani Inuit Association, she founded the summer camp Sprouts, a program for underprivileged youth in her community, when she was fifteen years old. She has worked as the executive assistant to Sheila Watt-Cloutier, the former president

of the Inuit Circumpolar Conference (www.inuitcircumpolar.com), and has recently completed a four-year term as chair of the Inuit Circumpolar Youth Council (www.niyc.ca). Miali has received recognition from the government of Nunavut for her work in promoting her first language, Inuktitut.

80

Annahid Dashtgard

I

T'S SEPTEMBER 2001. The twin towers have just tumbled, changing the world and my life as I know it. The racism directed at Middle Eastern people makes me feel like I'm eight years old again, when I first came to Canada and encountered hate. It's terrifying to face so much hostility and fear. To cope, I eat and purge more often: rocky road ice cream, honey-filled baklava, cheesecake. I eat them all and more to stuff my body with comfort—with love—and then get rid of it all in a ritual of control. As long as I can control my body, even in this brutal way, I feel that I can also control the world around me.

I've reached burnout. And I discover that the activist community I've contributed to for so long isn't there to support me when I need it most. I wonder: Why do I feel so disconnected from everyone around me when I've worked so hard to make the world a tighter, stronger community?

It's said that we're products of our histories. I lived the golden years of my childhood in Tehran. I remember mornings when I would wake with a jump and change into my purple daisy-printed swimsuit to dance for my adoring grandparents as they lay in bed. I can still picture the sun streaming through the window, high on the wall to my right. I revelled in the sensation of twirling faster and faster as my grandparents laughed harder and harder.

Then the dancing stopped. Fleeing the Iranian Revolution, my family moved to a town in Alberta, where I was hounded by racism and bullying, in school and within the larger community. I was spat on, I was chosen last—if at all—for teams, and kids began to taunt my younger siblings simply for being related to me. Meanwhile, my parents were struggling to make ends meet and integrate into a new society. They couldn't support me emotionally. I felt numb. I learned to hide my pain, fear, and unhappiness as I became desperate to win others' approval and fit in. I pushed away my emotions and my connection to my body.

I'd stopped dancing to my own rhythm; instead I did everything I could to conform to the people around me. This pattern would take me a long time and a lot of pain to break.

By university I had become an activist and I identified with the counterculture crowd. I didn't have a choice: I knew in my bones what injustice felt like, and I knew I had to fight back. After graduating, at the age of twenty-three, I got my first paid job as an activist with the provincial New Democratic Party. The Conservatives had just won the 1997 election. Their agenda of privatization and cutbacks caused a flood of phone calls to our offices—single mothers unable to cover childcare costs, families struggling with inadequate health care services, and civil service workers despairing over job losses or crushing workloads.

Stunned by the suffering around me, I started asking broader questions: Why is the government making decisions that clearly aren't in the public's interest? Who's really benefiting from its policies? A seasoned union organizer gave me some answers during lunch one day. He taught me about international trade agreements that transferred wealth from democratically elected governments to private investors and corporations. The North American Free Trade Agreement (NAFTA) was one of his many examples: while the Alberta government had cut millions from hospital budgets, significantly weakening our public health care system, NAFTA was opening the doors to private American health corporations that were eager to start offering for-profit services. Over a plate of french fries I began to see that the seemingly disparate kinds of despair I witnessed were really a product of power being concentrated in the hands of a small, unaccountable elite.

Thus, I began to learn about the devastating effect of corporate globalization on people around the world. I learned about people in Bolivia who couldn't afford drinking water after the government sold the public water system to an American company. I learned about farmers in India who could no longer plant their own crops because a U.S. corporation had patented the genes of their seeds. I learned about women in Indonesia locked in running-shoe factories who were beaten or fired if they dared unionize. I was enraged by the injustices being perpetuated in the name of free trade and was shocked to discover that Canada was far from innocent: at the time, our government was secretly negotiating the Multilateral Agreement on Investment (MAI), which proposed huge public policy—even constitutional—changes that threatened our public services, environment, and human rights record. The MAI would have allowed a private investor or corporation to sue our government if a democratically passed law limited their profits.

On a philosophical level it's clear to me now that the free trade movement—which was really about unfair, exploitative trade—is an expression of traditional masculine values, like competition and individuality, gone off the rails. I felt that free trade promoted an agenda of profit at any cost and ignored the common good.

After the Council of Canadians asked me to organize a national campaign against the MAI I immersed myself in social justice activism like never before. For five years I worked on trade justice across Canada—speaking at events, talking to media, chairing meetings, marching in demonstrations, writing reports, and sucking in more tear gas than I care to remember. I even emptied my life savings into producing a video called BYE-BUY WORLD: *The Battle of Seattle,* which was distributed to over five hundred universities, colleges, and non-profit and development organizations around the world. I committed my whole life to activism.

Yet, I had lost my balance. Throughout my teenage years, despite being a model student and extracurricular super-woman, I was an emotional mess. In my last years of high school I started using food as a way of coping with my emotions. I started binging and then purging. My childhood feelings of shame, sadness, and anger at being oppressed and bullied hadn't gone away but were coming out in self-destructive ways. And getting involved in activism didn't help my healing process at all. I thought if I worked hard enough I could eliminate some of the sources of major injustice in the world that cause people to hurt and oppress others as carelessly as children on the playground had done to me. I entered the urgent and addictive race to improve others' lives. I could never do enough; there was never any time to rest—other activists saw taking time off as a betrayal of our cause. The harder and faster I worked, the higher I rose in the activist pecking order.

The lack of balance in my life was taking its toll. I was destroying my body, and I could not control the physical consequences of my actions. In retrospect, I realize I was moving so fast I was starting to spin, disconnected from my innate rhythm and ignoring my dance. I was giving away more energy than I was getting back.

September 11 was the tipping point.

Six months after the tragedy I took out a last-minute booking for a four-month spiritual retreat at a yoga and health centre in the United States. There, sharing circles were a regular event: we learned to connect to ourselves by paying attention to our thoughts and feelings without judgment and to share those feelings with others whenever we felt compelled. What a revelation it was when I found that it was harder for me to speak from my heart to a handful of people I knew well than to deliver a speech to an auditorium packed with strangers. Halfway through my stay I took a huge step forward in my own healing: sitting on a picnic bench in the afternoon sun with the ten others in my group, I took a deep breath and admitted publicly that I struggled with an eating disorder.

Gradually, instead of swallowing my emotions with food, I learned more effective ways of expressing them. It astonished me that the process of searching for internal wholeness took just as much guts as fighting for justice in the outside world. At this point, in my late twenties, I started to rediscover my own rhythm, the steps to *my* dance. For a year I stopped thinking about healing the world to focus on connecting to and healing myself, and as a first step, I began training as a Zen shiatsu and reiki bodywork practitioner.

There was a saying we often used to greet each other at the

yoga centre: *Jai Bhagwan*, which we translated as, "I honour the God in you; I honour the light and dark in you." This saying moved me: I started to understand what it meant to accept both light and darkness, beauty and brutality, in myself and others. This understanding allowed me to change my relationship to myself and to the world of activism I'd left behind. I realized that to bring light to the various darknesses in the world, we need to first make peace with our own darkness— our own pain, sadness, and anger.

After a year I gradually began thinking about the outside world again. I realized that if I could combine my years of experience as a facilitator and educator on social justice issues with this healing work, I could push for social change in a way that would address inner emotional pain as well as external political injustices. Drawing from my own experience I began researching how women related to food and to their bodies. Very quickly, I verified my hunch that a majority—over three quarters—of North American women don't like their bodies, a feeling that is manifested in struggles with eating.

I learned that these struggles with food reflected emotional turmoil, a suppression of personal power or self-acceptance and perhaps, more fundamentally, a systematic denigration—in the media, politics, health care, education, and social services—of "feminine" values such as co-operation, sustainability, and interdependence. I knew of no programs that connected women's food struggles to both personal and political influences. So I decided to start one.

86 | I designed a Conscious Eating course for women struggling with food and their body image. Based on my research and my personal experiences, I sketched out ten areas I felt were crucial to women's sense of self, including spirituality, family history, and sexuality. I wanted my program to strengthen women's sense of self and personal power so that they wouldn't need to

abuse food as a coping mechanism and so that they could build a healthier society using their newly liberated energy. Once I'd finalized the course I made a simple flyer and posted it in cafés, health food stores, and libraries around Toronto.

Six women applied for the course's first run. In ten weeks I helped them become reacquainted with their emotions. At times it was heartbreaking. Some were bulimic and used food to purge their emotions, as I had. Another would eat herself into a comatose state every night. Yet another was anorexic. The participants were from a wide range of ages and ethnicities. But all struggled with the same basic problem of not feeling good enough. Some couldn't maintain eye contact while in the circle, and others were so stiff with shame that they couldn't move or weren't able to breathe while moving. Most were afraid to express their true thoughts publicly.

Throughout the course each woman practised self-awareness by paying close attention to her emotions through regular sharing circles, movement exercises, creative activities, and discussions of various relevant readings and videos. For these women, identifying their real feelings and then giving them voice was a terrifying process, but by learning the language of emotions, the language of the feminine, they were able to come home to their own bodies.

Reconnecting to our emotions is a radical, political process. I realized that emotions are what connect our personal experiences to the broader societal context. They link our inner and outer realities, our individual bodies to the global body. I deeply believe that the United States wouldn't have invaded Iraq if the American people had had the tools to cope with their fears and anger after 9/11.

At the end of the program I recorded feedback from course evaluations. The response was amazingly positive. The experience had provided these women with tools to deal with the problems in their daily lives. I too found myself at peace. As a new direction for my work became clear, I could see the purpose of all my years of struggle. I'd found a way to connect my own personal healing to my determination to make the world a better place.

Since that first course, I've worked with hundreds of girls and women from all sorts of backgrounds. I still run the Conscious Eating course and have expanded my work to offer courses focused on leadership and wellness. The most gratifying aspect of this new career path has been the feedback. The ratio of energy to reward has shifted dramatically, from the 90:10 of my activist years to 50:50 today. Women will often tell me—sometimes weeks, months, or years later—that some insight or teaching they learned in my course has made a radical difference in their lives. Following the program, they return not to their destructive relationship with food but to the ongoing journey of connecting with themselves and the greater sense of personal power that follows.

I know now that to achieve meaningful and long-lasting social change, it's important not only to change external conditions—unjust policies, laws, and practices; human rights abuses; exploitative trade agreements—but also to foster internal healing, because everything that we do in the world is a reflection of our inner selves. We need social justice activism more than ever before. Yet what I've discovered through my experiences is that the individuals and organizations working for social change need to find better ways to put their values into practice. Activist culture needs to clear more space for the heart, for emotional expression and support. Feeding ourselves images of injustice, suffering, and horror every day is hard on us. And when we don't deal with our emotions, they're unleashed in destructive actions towards ourselves and others. There's already so much division in the world that we're working to change; surely we don't need to reproduce it in our own circles.

Emma Goldman famously said, "If I can't dance, I don't want to be part of your revolution." And I say that finding our own inner rhythm, the steps to our own dance, is the only way there can ever be true revolution.

■ ■ ■ ■ ■

ANNAHID DASHTGARD is co-founder of Anima Leadership (www. animaleadership.com), a consulting and training organization that specializes in leadership, diversity, and gender issues. She continues to develop transformative educational programs that integrate emotional literacy with global justice education and has offered these programs across Canada as well as internationally. She currently lives in Toronto with her loving partner and many friends, a community without whom she would not be who she is now. She thanks her mother and grandmother for serving as role models for courage, strength, and boldness. She feels extremely blessed.

Ahmed Kayssi

I AM IRAQI. MY family lived in Baghdad, but when the Iraqi-Iranian war broke out in the early 1980s, life in the city became increasingly dangerous, and my parents decided to emigrate. I was only four when they sent my thirteen-year-old sister and me to stay with our grandmother in Cairo while they prepared to relocate permanently.

We settled in Saudi Arabia, where I grew up learning about my roots from my parents and got to know other cultures through the international schools that I attended. Iraq's influence on my childhood was largely through my parents' nostalgic reminiscences of the country's "glorious past"—the few years of peace that it enjoyed between the many wars and political upheavals that have shaped Iraq over the past century. Whatever relatives I had in Baghdad I only got to know through telephone conversations and infrequent summer reunions in Jordan, since we never returned to Iraq. My parents did not want to risk getting stuck there if Baghdad's airport were bombed or Iraq's borders were sealed for security reasons, which happened quite frequently in those days.

In Saudi Arabia my family and I were "foreign workers" living in the country on a temporary permit, and as an Iraqi I was automatically considered a stranger and, consequently, a member of a minority group.

My Iraqi heritage also affected the way that the local people and other foreigners living in Saudi Arabia reacted to me. Those who liked Iraq's then-president Saddam Hussein would heap praise on him when they recognized my Iraqi accent, while those who didn't like him, and they were a minority back then, would simply become cold or unfriendly, as if being Iraqi necessarily implied that I celebrated Saddam's leadership or condoned his many horrid humanitarian crimes.

A few years later, another war broke out when Saddam invaded Kuwait, and the entire world converged on the region to liberate the small Gulf state and its abundance of oil wells. Saudi Arabia joined the war against Iraq, which made living as an Iraqi in Saudi Arabia an awful situation. Some of our Iraqi friends were deported or harassed until they packed up and left. My personal experience was not markedly different. A few of my Saudi classmates decided to do their patriotic duty by unleashing their adolescent aggression on the only Iraqi they knew—me.

For the next several months, I was known as "the Iraqi," and my peers excluded me from social functions and berated me for my country's evil and wickedness. My sister, who was at university at the time, was luckier in the sense that her social circle was more mature, but I still remember the day she came home with a "gift" that she got from a classmate: a gory graphic book about Iraqi "crimes" in Kuwait with a note warning her that our transgressions would never be forgotten.

Eventually, the Iraqi occupation of Kuwait ended, and life returned to normal, but my parents decided to immigrate to Canada a few years later so that we would never have to relive the stress we faced during the war. In Canada my attachment to Iraq grew weaker, because my ethnic background didn't matter as much as it did in the Middle East. Being Iraqi, or Greek or Scottish, wasn't as important in Canada as the way one carried oneself and interacted with others. As long as I respected the country's diversity of opinions and lifestyles, observed the laws of the land, and worked hard, I felt I would be treated with respect and could achieve wonderful things. In essence, for the first time in my life I felt I was accepted as an equal, and I began to love this country as my own.

My childhood experiences have affected enormously how I've developed as an adult, and my story is in no way unique: my Arab friends and I have often struggled with memories of our experiences growing up in a world that was full of prejudice. We eventually concluded that the biggest problem facing the Middle East today was not that our leaders were corrupt or that our societies were lawless, but that our youth desperately lacked role models to inspire and guide them as they navigated a world in which those living beyond our borders, particularly in the West, perceived everything Arab and Islamic as crooked and undesirable. We thus decided to become the role models that we so longingly sought. We wanted to inspire: to learn as much as possible from our Canadian communities and pass on that knowledge to future generations back home so that they can build a more progressive society.

And so I immersed myself in my new Canadian home as much as I could. I attended Queen's University and became heavily involved in student government. I wanted to understand what made people here so tolerant compared with people in other parts of the world. I acknowledge that prejudices still exist in Canada against First Nations groups and those with different cultural backgrounds or sexual preferences. But all its flaws notwithstanding, Canadian society is still a vast improvement over anything I had experienced in the Middle East or during my travels in Europe.

I helped start the Queen's Arab Students Association with the aim of bringing Arab students together and introducing them to the many things a Canadian university campus has to offer. I took courses in critical thinking, creative writing, logic, and ethics just to expand my mind, and I encouraged everyone I knew to do the same. I ran for positions in student government, both in residence and in various campus groups, and eventually I won the rectorship of Queen's, the highest student office at the university, becoming the first person from a visible ethnic minority to hold that post in the school's history.

Every year or so, I would go back to visit family in the Middle East, and during my time there I would always try to challenge people I met with new ideas or concepts. If they were conservative and religious, I would point out the intrinsic hypocrisies in many modern interpretations of Islam, and there was certainly never a problem finding an inconsistency in how people interpreted our faith back home; for example, all of my strictly religious friends would shudder at the idea of drinking alcohol or eating pork, but many would routinely talk about people behind their backs or make unfair generalizations about groups they didn't like, as if good manners weren't as integral to the Islamic faith as rituals and culinary rules. If they were nationalistic, I would bring attention to the folly of their ideal of the nation-state in a part of the world where international borders had been drawn by colonial masters rather than by national consensus. If they were anti-Western, I would invite them to boycott American media, music, or even McDonald's food for even a week, knowing full well that most of them would never contemplate taking such a step. Yes, I often came across as a killjoy, but I was careful never to go too far, and my aim was always simply to get people to question the status quo. If they were uncomfortable with my questions, all the better, because it meant that they were starting to think.

At school I tried hard to get students new to Canada, wherever they came from, to take advantage of the opportunities available at Queen's, whether it be in athletics, on-campus jobs, or cultural or political clubs. I found that appealing to self-interest was always the best way of getting people involved: "Join the debating club because it'll look really good on your résumé when you apply to grad school!" usually worked a lot better than "As a debater you will learn a lot of valuable skills in public speaking and argumentation." I tried not to judge people's motivations, but I was happy if they experimented with a club or activity that was a complete departure from anything they would have considered pursuing in their home countries.

Some of these students did not continue in their extra-curricular pursuits because they got bored or were simply not interested. But many did, and eventually there was a significant number of extremely active students from all over the world doing amazing things at Queen's. The student government elected an Australian friend of mine as a speaker of its assembly, the same post that Peter Milliken, current Speaker of the House of Commons, once held, and a few years ago the vice-president of the student government was a Norwegian student I had met in his first week at Queen's. And students from Arab, Chinese, or Indian backgrounds became increasingly involved in the Queen's residences, the engineering society, and a variety of prominent clubs on campus.

Although it would be extremely inaccurate and presumptuous to suggest that I am responsible for this movement, I do occasionally encounter people in their final year at Queen's who would tell me that a conversation we had in their first year got them interested in a particular activity that they subsequently became heavily involved in. Such anecdotes make me truly happy, because they mean that I was able to make a difference in a person's life.

That is my form of activism in a nutshell, the activism that quietly seeks out the individual, makes him or her uncomfortable with the status quo, and challenges that person to change his or her perspective on the world. It is very personal and unglamorous. It does not involve speeches or organizing political movements and rallies. Instead I share long meals, go out for coffee or tea, or chat with people whenever possible. I try never to lose hope in the potential of anyone to do anything they passionately want to do. I maintain this optimism and support because when I was a teenager enduring the most challenging time of my life in Saudi Arabia, I desperately wanted to meet someone who would inspire me in that same way. And I cannot help but think that if enough Iraqis and Arabs in the Middle East and beyond inspired one another, then maybe, just maybe, our war-torn part of the world can begin the tortuous journey towards recovery.

■ ■ ■ ■ ■

AHMED KAYSSI moved to Canada from the Middle East with his family in 1996. He has been a Queen's University student since 1998: he completed a dual degree in engineering chemistry and business German and a master's degree in physiology. He is currently enrolled in Queen's Medical School. Ahmed founded the Queen's Arab Students Association and worked with numerous student groups at Queen's before serving as the University's twenty-eighth rector. He hopes to train as a surgeon.

FREE THE CHILDREN:
THE WORLD'S LARGEST
NETWORK OF CHILDREN
HELPING CHILDREN
THROUGH EDUCATION

Craig Kielburger

SOME OF LIFE'S turning points are visible miles ahead and can be planned for meticulously in advance. Others appear out of nowhere, taking you by surprise and changing everything. My journey as a child rights activist began with this second kind of turning point.

It all started one ordinary Wednesday morning when I was twelve. As usual, I raced downstairs for breakfast determined to read the comics before leaving for school. As far as I was concerned there was no better way to start the day. As I flipped past the sections of the newspaper I never read, a headline jumped out at me: "Battled child labor, boy, 12, murdered." This boy was exactly my age. Suddenly, the comics didn't seem so important any more.

Curious, I sat down to read the article. That's when I first learned about the life and death of Iqbal Masih, a former child labourer—turned—child rights activist. Appalled, I read about the brutal conditions under which Iqbal had worked for much of his short life. Sold into slavery at the age of four, the Pakistani boy had spent six years chained to a carpet-weaving loom before making a miraculous escape,and becoming an advocate for the rights of enslaved children everywhere. His awareness campaign about child labour captured the world's attention, prompting a carpet maker to have him killed.

Iqbal's story shocked me, a middle-class grade seven student from Thornhill, Ontario. I could hardly believe that although Iqbal and I were the same age, our lives were so radically different. Until then I'd taken so much for granted—loving parents and a fantastic older brother, supportive teachers, and lots of good friends. I looked forward to new toys, family vacations, and after-school sports. Like every other kid I knew, I went to school five days a week and spent Saturday and Sunday having fun. Of course I'd seen suffering on TV, in the newspaper, and even walking past homeless people downtown. But like most people, I'd learned to tune it out.

Reading Iqbal's story made me angry. It seemed incredibly unfair that Iqbal had had to endure such terrible treatment and then be killed for speaking up, while I'd been lucky enough to be born into a happy family and affluent community. To be honest, I don't think I fully understood injustice until I saw it through the eyes of another twelve-year-old. At that point, all my certainties about the world evaporated. I had so many questions: What kind of people would sell their son? How could anybody get away with keeping a child prisoner? What exactly was child labour?

I headed to the library as soon as I could to find some answers. As I began to research child labour I made a horrific discovery: in many parts of the world, children exactly like me were forced to spend their days working in the most awful conditions. While I sat in class millions of children would only ever dream of going to school. It seemed unbelievable that I'd never heard about any of this before. I wondered if I was the only one.

It didn't take long for me to decide that I needed to share what I'd learned. The hardest part was finding the courage to speak to my class. Although I was generally outgoing, public speaking was definitely not my favourite activity. I can still remember how nervous I felt standing up at the front of my classroom and how quiet everyone became as I began to share what I knew about Iqbal and the plight of other child labourers. As I spoke, I could sense that others were equally horrified. When I asked my class who wanted to help these kids, I wasn't sure what would happen. But before I knew it, hands flew up. That's when it first dawned on me that having the courage to try makes even the most difficult things possible.

Later a group of us sat down to discuss our next move, and it was then that Free The Children was born. None of us had much experience with social justice work, and my only qualification was my desire to make a difference. I wanted to channel my shock and anger about child labour into meaningful action.

In the beginning Free The Children's main goal was to raise awareness about the situation facing child labourers. One of our first projects was to create a display for a local youth fair. I still remember how we arrived with our lovingly decorated sheets of cardboard to find that everyone else had slick, professional-looking displays. This event may have been a youth fair, but most of the participants were adults. At the time—more than ten years ago—youth activism had yet to come into its own. Children's opinions were rarely heard, and their interests were almost always represented by adults. As children speaking out on children's rights, we were an oddity. Curious people flocked to our table just to hear what we had to say. It was then that we began to realize how important it was for us, as children, to have a voice of our own. By speaking up we were breaking new ground.

Soon, Free The Children started to expand the scope of its activities. While working to free children from labour and exploitation by raising awareness about the issue at home and appealing to governments in developing countries to make laws to curtail child labour, we also sought to free our peers around the world from the idea that we were too young to bring about positive change. This campaign was to be an uphill battle.

Although our families and friends were always right there cheering us on, and ever willing to lend a hand, other adults were generally skeptical about what we could accomplish. I still remember how one person told me he "would rather hear the message from my father." Another actually went so far as to say, "Children should be seen and not heard!" Whenever we approached existing organizations, all they wanted us to do was convince our parents to make a donation. The fact that we were often dismissed as "just a bunch of kids" was incredibly frustrating—and it hurt. Yet it also strengthened our resolve. We became all the more determined to show that children could actually help children. With adults unwilling to get involved, we started to make connections with the one group we knew would understand: other young people.

Before long I was speaking to groups everywhere about child labour. And audiences were actually interested in what I had to say. When I spoke at events people would often ask whether I'd ever actually met any child labourers. Sometimes they would imply that without first-hand experience, I couldn't really claim to understand the situation. This set me thinking,

"What better way to find out how to help child labourers than to ask the children themselves?" There was only one problem: I wasn't even allowed to take the subway by myself, much less cross international borders. I wasn't certain how I was going to convince my parents to let me travel halfway across the globe.

By a stroke of luck, a family friend, Alam Rahman, was planning a trip to South Asia at that time and generously invited me along. My parents trusted Alam, and before I knew it the trip of a lifetime was taking shape. We arranged to meet Alam in Dhaka, Bangladesh, where we would begin a seven-week tour of Bangladesh, Nepal, India, Pakistan, and Thailand.

Although I tried to learn all I could about South Asia before my trip, I don't think anything could have prepared me for the experience of actually being there. From the moment Alam and I left the airport in a rickshaw, it was clear that we were in a different world. From the beginning we agreed that there would be no time to waste. One of the first places we visited was a sprawling slum just outside the city.

In the blistering heat of that afternoon I saw poverty up close. Children clad only in dirty rags ran up to us full of curiosity, their distended bellies speaking of extreme malnutrition. Homes consisted of little more than bits of scavenged cardboard and corrugated tin precariously pieced together. Paths were littered with all kinds of refuse, even human waste. There wasn't a school, a hospital, or even anything that looked like a building anywhere in sight.

By the time we arrived for our appointment with a local human rights worker, I hardly knew what to say. The only question I managed to ask him was, "How can I help?" To my surprise he told me to go back home—and describe to my friends the deprivation and suffering I'd witnessed. He encouraged me to ask them whether it was fair that some people have so little in our world of plenty and whether it was fair that one of the reasons places like this slum exist is because of the choices people in our country make.

This advice echoed in my head during my time in South Asia. I met many children with so little, most of whom worked in the worst possible conditions. I'd expected child labour to be a shameful secret, difficult to uncover, but everywhere we went children were out working in plain view. It was all too easy to find child labourers to talk to. In Thailand I met with eleven-year-old prostitutes who'd grown up in brothels. In India I met children who'd spent their entire lives making bricks out of mud. In a remote factory I spoke to an eight-year-old girl whose job was to pull apart used syringes so that the parts could be sold. Medical waste covered the floor where she sat. She was surrounded by piles of bloodied needles but wore neither shoes nor gloves. She'd never heard of AIDS.

During my trip I continually struggled to come to terms with what I was witnessing. Every day I was sickened by the things that children had to do to survive and angry that they didn't have the opportunities they deserved. Again and again, I heard that parents didn't want to send their child to work, and time after time I was told it was the only means of survival for the poor. Children told me that they had no choice but to work. They explained how hard they struggled, hoping for a better future. I was awed by their resilience and courage. I was also amazed by their capacity for kindness and fun. In the most desperate places children eagerly shared their stories with us. At times we even found ourselves laughing and playing together, engrossed in a game of tag or a tickle war.

Although we were never in one place for long, I made many new friends during that trip. I desperately wanted to help each of the children I came to know. I yearned to instantly ensure that each one could enjoy the basic necessities of life. Often I felt frustrated by how little I could actually do to help them through the day. Slowly I came to realize that the advice the human rights worker in Bangladesh gave me had been on the mark. The one way that a twelve-year-old from Canada could really make a difference was by sharing these children's stories and explaining their plight to others. I could return their friendship and generosity by making certain they would never be forgotten.

In South Asia I had the chance to talk with some of the world's poorest children and learn about their struggles. In the process I came to see child labour as both the cause and consequence of poverty. I began to acknowledge that it wasn't enough to simply be against child labour when children and their families were desperately in need of basic necessities and new opportunities. During my travels I came to understand that freeing children meant more than ensuring that no child be enslaved—it meant empowering young people and their families. By the end of my trip, it had become clear that Free The Children had a lot of work to do.

At that point even I didn't know the extent to which my trip would subsequently shape the direction of my life. Almost as soon as I returned to Canada life in our Thornhill house changed forever. Requests for information started to pour in, with students from across the country wanting to know how they could become involved with Free The Children. We were flooded with speaking requests, and people from all walks of life began to ask how they could support our work. It was at this point that Free The Children began to gain the momentum that sustains it today.

I still find it hard to believe that Free The Children has grown from a small group of classmates into the world's largest network of children helping children. Once an after-school group, we are now a registered charity with field operations around the world. Still, in a lot of ways, things haven't really changed. We remain as determined as ever to build a better world, and we still live this commitment through projects that we plan one by one. Only now, a network that once consisted of a few Canadian students encompasses Youth in Action groups around the globe involving more that 100,000 young people in their annual campaigns. Education, always at the centre of our work, has taken on new importance over the years. We're now committed to both educating people about a variety of issues that affect children and youth and enabling children around the world to benefit from primary education. Today we implement projects in several developing countries, convinced that education programs must empower families to meet their basic needs.

Ten years later I am still driven by the commitment I made on my first trip to South Asia: to ensure that the plight of the world's children will never be forgotten. Over time I have come to understand that this commitment must involve empowering a new generation of social activists back home.

Since 1999 my brother, Marc, and I have been able to work towards this goal through Leaders Today, a youth leadership training organization. Each year we connect with 250,000 young people across North America who use our *Take Action!* textbooks in schools and participate in our leadership training programs, which include seminars, camps, and week-long academies. Our intention has always been not only to involve young people already committed to social justice but also to reach out to the wider population in order to bring about lasting change on a larger scale. And it's happening. Whether it's a student volunteer ambassador in Ontario or British

Columbia helping classmates fulfill their required community involvement hours through the Volunteer Now! program, a social issues club in Calgary supporting development projects through our Adopt a Village fundraising program, or one of the six hundred youth annually who travel to China, India, Kenya, Ecuador, Mexico, and Thailand to volunteer in a developing country, young people are making their voices heard and their actions count.

As for me, in my role as founder and chair of Free The Children, I've now travelled to more than fifty countries around the world, visiting underprivileged children, speaking out about children's rights, and inspecting our many projects. I've had the honour of opening Free The Children's first school and recently joined in celebrating the construction of our 450th. I've been fortunate enough to speak with a few of the 500,000 people who've benefited from our health care centres and witnessed how young people's efforts to bring clean water and sanitation systems to remote villages have contributed to the well-being of entire communities. I've also had the chance to examine the progress of Free The Children's alternative income projects and interview participants who've been able to remove their children from dangerous working conditions. Although I've also had the privilege of meeting with a number of the world's most powerful political and spiritual leaders, it is the encounters with children and families that have affected me the most. Whenever I speak with a new student or a proud parent, a recovering patient or a dedicated community leader, I am reminded that change is possible. If I begin to feel daunted by the magnitude of some challenge, these are the people I remember.

HAILING FROM TORONTO, Ontario, Craig Kielburger founded the human rights organization Free The Children (www.freethechildren. com) when he was twelve and later co-founded the youth leader-ship training organization Leaders Today (www.leaderstoday.com) as well as Me to We (www.metowe.org), an organization that encourages its members to improve their world by reaching out to others. Along with his brother, Marc, Craig has worked to eliminate child labour and promote youth leadership around the world, and his efforts earned him the World Children's Prize for the Rights of the Child in 2006. Free The Children is now the world's largest network of children helping children. Craig has written or co-written several books, including *Free The Children, Take Action: A Guide to Active Citizenship, Take More Action,* and *Me to We: Finding Meaning In a Material World.*

REASONS TO DREAM

Jessica Lax

WHEN I MEET people who are working towards a just and sustainable future, I like to ask about their tipping points. For some of them, becoming socially and environmentally conscious took time; when I picture their tipping points I imagine pebbles building up on a teeter-totter, eventually forming a pile big enough to tip these individuals towards realizing that their actions make a difference. For others, their conscientiousness came from a single life-altering experience. It's as if a boulder dropped on one end of their teeter-totters, catapulting them towards awareness of the world around them. These pebbles and boulders might be a passionate speech, a powerful book, or an all-night conversation with an inspiring friend.

I reached a tipping point when I was twenty-one. I'd been accumulating pebbles for a few years—I had started to recognize that I had a connection to the world and a responsibility to make it better. But that year I had a transformative experience. A huge boulder fell among the pebbles when I took a trip to East Africa.

I went to Kenya through the Canadian Field Studies in Africa program with about seventy other university students. For a semester we journeyed throughout the country, visiting cities and villages, setting up camp in a difference place every week. As we travelled we completed courses in subjects ranging from agroforestry to anthropology. I'd travelled a lot before and wasn't expecting a dramatic, life-changing experience. But I came home with a new outlook, a new lifestyle, and a new life plan.

Our group went on daily field trips in big green army trucks. Our caravan passed through rural villages devastated by deforestation and desertification: cows no longer had grazing land, and people were unable to grow their own food. In urban slums we saw row upon row of houses made of corrugated steel and cardboard, with garbage and sewage lining the pathways. We also visited international development projects that had done a lot of harm despite good intentions: a donated fish cannery in Lake Turkana sat unused because fish populations dropped suddenly from over-fishing; villages all over Kenya were stuck with tractors they had been given that had since broken down; and we met children who had been removed from their nomadic families to attend school in northern Kenya only to learn about British history and industry because the school had no educational resources beyond donated British textbooks. I was bombarded by images of wasted potential. It seemed to me that poverty and its causes ran so deep that a solution simply couldn't exist.

I also experienced a clash of cultures unlike anything I'd ever felt before. Everywhere we went we travelled in a

North American bubble, and I was constantly reminded of my privilege back home. As I heard some students complain that dinner was late or that the showers were cold, I could see local people with nothing to eat and barely enough to drink watching us through the campsite fence. Some students would come back from markets and boast about the incredible bargains they'd got from desperate people. The advantages we enjoyed where we stayed—the swimming pools, the beer—all seemed normal within the bubble, but in the context of the poverty I saw on our daily field trips the clash was obscene.

After seeing starving children who followed my every step begging for food, I wasn't in the mood to unwind for a good time when evening came. Instead I contemplated my place in the global community and wrote in my journal about what I saw and how I felt. I suddenly grasped the sheer injustice of the growing gap between rich and poor the world over.

My emotions ran the gamut from anger, resentment, and confusion to powerlessness, guilt, and despair. No matter how much I tried to rationalize why I was able to live in an affluent part of the globe, I just couldn't justify the existence of two such different, unequal worlds. I couldn't ignore the guilt that I felt for being so privileged. My guilt also came with a sense of responsibility to work towards equality, but I couldn't see how I could achieve this goal.

I wasn't the only one in my group who felt this way. Some of the other students and I deconstructed the ways that we, in our lives back home, were perpetuating the problems we saw around us. In these discussions, I felt a particular kinship to a young woman named Jocelyn Land-Murphy. Together we dissected every aspect of our lives and realized that many of our actions deemed acceptable by our society—buying unfairly traded products, consuming much more than we needed,

driving cars when we didn't need to—had destructive consequences. This process was extremely difficult for both of us, as
we quickly discovered how much our daily lives undermined
the positive future we passionately wanted to build. How
could we talk about ending child poverty when we buy clothes
from companies that employ children in horrendous working
conditions? How could we lament the plight of people earning
minuscule wages when we choose not to buy fair trade coffee
back in Canada? As we analyzed the implications of our everyday choices, Jocelyn and I continued to challenge and support
one another, and one of the strongest friendships of my life
started to develop.

This critical analysis empowered us by showing us how we
were connected to the rest of the world. Yes, we were contributing to the exploitation of resources, people, and other species with our consumerist lifestyles, but we also had the power
to alter our lifestyles and make choices that would foster a culture of respect—for all of our planet's inhabitants and for the
earth itself.

Once we understood that the poverty and environmental
degradation we saw in Kenya was connected to our lifestyles
back home, we realized that the biggest problem wasn't in
Kenya or other developing countries, but in our own culture
of excessive consumption. I knew I had to act immediately
to help solve this problem, and I came to believe that I could
be most effective by helping my peers—young Canadians—
change *their* lifestyles and consumer patterns, which would in
turn benefit everyone, including Kenyans.

With this aim in mind Jocelyn and I founded the Otesha
Project. Otesha means "reason to dream" in Swahili, one of
Kenya's native languages, and we chose this word because it
represented our own change in consciousness and communicated our message of empowerment and hope. We dreamed

up a plan to cycle across Canada, from school to school, town to town, to give presentations about the power we all have to make positive change through our everyday choices. We wanted to drop as many pebbles, or boulders, as possible.

After a tremendous amount of planning, our first cross-country trip began in May 2003. Together with thirty-one other people our age, Jocelyn and I biked from Vancouver, B.C., to Corner Brook, Newfoundland. Over twelve thousand people attended our presentations. One of the main features is a play that highlights all the choices we make between 8:00 and 9:00 AM. One character, Careless Consumer, takes a long shower, wears clothes made in a sweatshop, watches loads of TV, orders coffee in a Styrofoam cup, eats fast food, and drives to school. Careless understands her choices but makes them anyway, convinced that one person can't make a difference. Another character, Hopeful Hooligan, chooses to conserve water, wear sweatshop-free clothing, turn off the TV, drink fair trade coffee in a reusable mug, seek out organic and vegetarian food, and bus or bike to school. Mother Earth, the third character, chides Careless and cheers on Hopeful while offering background information on water, trade, waste, media, food, and transportation issues. Along with a crew of human props, Mother Earth also provides comic relief by wearing a frilly 1950s-style dress, breaking out in song, dance, or rap, and dropping jokes about reusable containers being the best thing since compost.

We use this one hour of the morning as an example of the hundreds of choices we make every day and, therefore, the hundreds of opportunities we have to take action to better our world.

As we travelled across the country the energy of the Otesha team attracted everyone from curious passersby to grocery store clerks to new bike-team members. Young people across Canada were drawn to our idealistic but confident belief in a better world. After our presentations students shared with us their new-found inspiration and commitment to action. Sandy from Nelson, B.C., said she found our message very empowering and wrote, "Since seeing your presentation I have not driven my car in three months! I have opted instead for bikes and buses." Thirteen-year-old Carolynne said that the Otesha Project "really shows you that everything you do has an impact on the world and it makes you want to do what you can to change that." And Danyela, an eighteen-year-old student, wrote, "I was lucky enough to be present as the two people came to talk to our class about the Otesha Project and inspired youth to stand up and have a say. The results were very eye-opening and made me think twice about how I live my life. It was motivating to feel a sense of power as a youth and to stand up for what should be changed."

We began to realize the unstoppable power of having a group of young, vibrant people dance into a venue bringing with them energy, ideas, and encouragement. And as people got excited, jumped on their feet, and joined in, they re-energized and re-empowered Jocelyn and me to keep working towards our dream.

We realized that young people in this country don't have many positive role models and that they're drowning in doomsday messages from media that report on problems but not solutions. One seven-year-old told us he had no hope. Being able to show people that there *are* solutions they can put in practice, that there is hope, gave us an incredible buzz. We realized how important it was to show that specific, tangible, and practical everyday actions make a real difference and are essential to kick-starting a cycle of action and empowerment.

When Jocelyn and I first got home and started researching and testing our new ideas, we were fuelled by our emotional reaction to our trip to Kenya—and our shock on returning to our culture of affluence and waste. We were swept along by our feelings of guilt and responsibility and the urgent need to be part of the solution rather than the problem. We worked tirelessly, never forgetting the people and experiences that prompted us to question how we lived. Today we're still energized by our reaction to our trip, but it's seeing Otesha's positive impact that motivates us to keep working for change. The barrage of emails, postcards, and responses we got after our presentations inspired us to search for ways to reach even more people with our message.

In 2005 Otesha organized three regional bicycle tours and one national tour. We wrote and self-published *The Otesha Book: From Junk to Funk,* which explores the social justice and environmental issues in our presentations but in much greater detail. Through our Hopeful High-School Hooligans (Triple-H) program ten teams of incredible high-school students across Ontario give presentations about responsible choices in their own communities. The Otesha Project is now a registered charity with hundreds of active members who are spreading awareness and hope every day. We're now planning to expand our bicycle tours throughout the country and reach even more communities in the summers to come.

My work with the Otesha Project has given me proof that change can, does, and will happen. I can pinpoint hundreds of moments where I witnessed a tipping point first-hand: a team member's dad trading in his SUV for a hybrid car; a group of students campaigning to get fair trade chocolate in their cafeteria; kids in Creston, B.C., running to tell us they'd biked to school that day; a young woman running her own bike trip; a couple in Sydney, Nova Scotia, renewing their lobbying efforts for a bike-friendly city; a young woman in Edmonton excitedly telling us how she'd been taking staggered showers and "letting the yellow mellow" rather than flushing the toilet.

I can see the Otesha bike tour members analyzing their life choices and donating their energy to improving the lives of others. I can see the teams of Hopeful High-School Hooligans taking the Otesha theatre production and making it their own, their cynicism fading and their hope growing as they realize that they can make a positive contribution to the world. I can see the hundreds of organizations we have met with who are doing amazing world-changing work every day. I can see people carrying around Tupperware containers, declining store bags when they make purchases, turning off lights, discussing the ethics of cheese, giving random hugs and spreading joy, pulling out hankies, resisting the pressure to consume more than they need, and questioning stereotypes. I can see people living consciously, making connections between their choices and the impacts of those choices, and then acting on those connections . . . I can see piles of pebbles building and boulders dropping all over the place.

When I look in the mirror I see a very different person from the young woman who went to Kenya. I see the hundreds of changes I've made in my own life and the pride, power, amazement, love, confidence, and inspiration I've helped foster in others. It's extremely fulfilling to wake up in the morning and take part in a movement to build a better world. I know there's nothing I'd rather be doing, because nothing would give me more hope. In Kenya a boulder fell, transforming my powerlessness into power. Four years on I know my life has changed for good.

JESSICA LAX is from Ottawa, Ontario, and holds a B.A. in biology and geography from Bishop's University in Quebec. She has also studied at Rhodes University in South Africa and with the Canadian Field Studies Program in Kenya. Jessica, along with Jocelyn Land-Murphy, co-founded the Otesha Project (www.otesha.ca). In 2003 they coordinated Otesha's first cross-Canada bike tour, and in 2005, Otesha published *The Otesha Book: From Junk to Funk,* available in both English and French. Jessica and Jocelyn have won multiple awards for their work, including a YouthActionNet award, Environment Canada's Cambio scholarship, the Tooker Gomberg award, and, most recently, the EECOM award for excellence in environmental education. Jessica continues to act as a director of the Otesha Project and is intimately involved with the organization's many ongoing programs across the country.

Shakil Choudhury

THE SUN IS streaming in the through the sliding glass doors, giving the teak wood of the kitchen cabinet a golden glow. The sound of eggs frying on the stovetop—loaded *desi*-style with tomatoes, onions, paprika, and coriander—draws us into the kitchen. We see my mum preparing, one by one, warm durum flour *parathas* stuffed with potatoes and white radish. Siblings, uncles, aunts, nieces, nephews, and grandparents crowd around the kitchen table with cups of hot chai in hand as the spicy, mouth-watering aromas wrap around us. Inevitably, the stories begin—sparkling, wondrous jewels for my sisters and me. My father and Shamim Aunty are exquisite storytellers. They tell us about the past when they were young and invincible, about our near and distant relatives, or about the trials and tribulations of their journeys during the India-Pakistan partition. I love these gatherings: the food, the family, the stories. But I didn't always.

Like many Canadian kids of colour, I grew up ashamed of my "brownness." Being of South Asian heritage, I had always struggled to find my place in Canadian society. If you had asked me what I thought of my life when I was in high school, I would have told you that I was a happy, well-adjusted student. My actions, however, suggested otherwise. I was embarrassed by our food, I cringed at the thick accents of my parents' imperfect English, and most telling, I avoided associating with other South Asians.

All that time I couldn't see that I was fighting myself. I didn't have the language or ability to recognize, let alone describe, the feelings of inferiority I wrestled with. This shame went on from when I was very young to my twenties. It wasn't until I started pursuing my master's degree at York University that I made the connections between my personal experiences and the bigger forces at work in Canadian society.

I began to explore how racism and oppression shaped our society's power structure. I learned that the financial elite and corporate sector controlled many of our political and economic policies; that studies, government reports, and commissions repeatedly demonstrated that there was, and still is, both subtle and overt racism throughout Canada's institutions, like the disproportionately high incarceration rates for Aboriginals perpetuated by a predominantly white police and judicial system; that statistical and qualitative analyses proved that visible minorities, women, and other marginalized groups are systematically denied equitable access to jobs, pay, and other societal resources. It was amazing for me to learn that there was even a term to describe my childhood feelings of cultural shame and rejection—"internalized racism"—and that it was a phenomenon common among members of visible minorities.

The quantity and clarity of information was overwhelming. I felt shocked, furious—and transformed—by what I learned.

I trained as a teacher and had been working in education for a few years at this point, and I was stunned that I had never heard about this systemic racism before. Why weren't governments and society at large doing more to fix the problems? At the very least, why didn't the media discuss these issues *loudly* every day? What was happening to justice, truth, and compassion?

I couldn't help but feel as though we, as citizens, were being systematically misinformed by the powers that be: our media, government, education system. I wanted to break this destructive pattern, to create something that offered real, lived experiences—stories—that would broaden perspectives and shatter stereotypes.

I'd grown up without role models or stories that could help my Canadian identity connect with my South Asian ethnicity. I had heard my family tell their personal stories, but I didn't know where they fit in my life as a Canadian. I wanted to know about South Asians—not from a historical Gandhi-British-Raj kind of way, but from a contemporary, lived, Canadian perspective. I was an active volunteer—I worked with the elderly in hospitals, served on student councils, and worked with youth development organizations—and I wanted to meet other civic-minded South Asians who were striving to make their communities better places. It was important for me to connect not just with young South Asian–Canadians but also with those who lived in South Asia, where my family's cultural and historical roots are planted. It was this realization that inspired the project called *The Brown Book: Voices of Young Pakistani and Muslim Activists from Toronto and Lahore.*

IT'S THE SPRING of 1996, and I'm in Lahore, Pakistan. I'm riding on the back of Mushtaq's motorcycle, weaving through the city's dusty streets late at night. We stop often so that he can share with me highlights of the Lahori "nightlife": a park in the middle of a traffic roundabout where hundreds of male labourers gather each night to sleep on the soft grass; street corners where prostitutes dressed as modest women in burkas wait to be picked up; the city's late-night eateries.

I'd only been in Pakistan for a week doing research for *The Brown Book* when I met Mushtaq. I was extremely grateful when he offered to be my personal guide to Lahore. Our frequent motorcycle rides allowed us to compare our lives—the politics of our respective home countries, the choices, challenges, and successes of our professional and personal lives, as well as our hopes for the future. One of the most principled individuals I've ever met, Mushtaq eventually became a dear, lifelong friend.

I was inspired to learn about the work Mushtaq's organization, Insan Foundation, was pioneering with child labourers. Using theatre as well as interactive, child-friendly learning techniques, they aimed to empower and educate illiterate children and teenagers who worked in factories, auto shops, and other hazardous facilities. I heard the stories of these young people: they endured long hours, horrible wages, verbal abuse, beatings, and broken bones at the hands of their employers. For them it was a turning point to connect with Insan Foundation, not only to learn to read and write, but also to discover that it was *not* okay for them to be treated with the cruelty they faced in their work environments, that as humans they deserved more dignity. In their own words they described discovering self-respect and increased confidence and feeling equipped to make healthier choices in their lives.

This story was one of many that I heard during the research stage of *The Brown Book*, where I discovered young people from Toronto and Lahore working on projects to promote gender equity, anti-racism, and human rights. Meeting

118

these ordinary young people who shared a Pakistani/Muslim background—my heritage—was inspiring and affirming. My conversations with them helped break down the stereotypes I carried about my own people. Their stories made me feel proud and rooted for the first time as both a Canadian and a South Asian.

In the fall of 2000, after a year of fundraising and grant writing, I managed to independently publish *The Brown Book*. My dear friend Chris Hayward did the graphic design and layout, and a host of individuals and organizations, including the Canadian Race Relations Foundation, the Elementary Teachers' Federation of Ontario, and South Asia Partnership–Pakistan, supported my project in a variety of ways, providing contacts, guidance, and funding.

When *The Brown Book* came out, there was an immediate demand from the school boards for a facilitator's guide to show teachers how to use it in the classroom. The skills I'd nurtured in the voluntary sector coupled with my experience as an educator helped me put together an effective anti-racist program for teachers. I used my personal story as well as *The Brown Book* as a springboard for discussion about racism, bias, and equality. I encouraged the workshop participants to describe their views of Muslim and South Asian people. They consistently responded with negative and exotic terms—"terrorists," "veils," "spicy food," and "Bollywood"—a pattern that made plain Canadian society's limited understanding and systemic bias towards people of my ethno-cultural and religious tradition. I then used the positive stories from *The Brown Book* to challenge the stereotypes about Muslim and South Asian people.

The feedback, on the workshop evaluations and through the participants' anecdotes, was tremendous. People were beginning to understand bias—their own as well as society's—and saw issues of racism and equality in new and meaningful ways.

Jimmy, a student in one of my anti-racism workshops, wasn't so different from me when I was his age. He was of South Asian ethnicity, he doubted himself and his identity, and he'd developed a remarkable ability to be "normal"—right down to his name. Rejecting his birth name, Jamshid, he'd encouraged people to call him Jimmy from an early age. Through *The Brown Book* workshop Jimmy started to recognize how racism affected him, and he discovered the origins of his shame about his ethno-cultural background. When I shared my story of growing up ashamed and confused about my identity, Jimmy became very quiet and withdrawn. In a conversation he had later with his teacher and mentor, he revealed that his experiences were similar to mine. The presentation spoke to him directly, and he was moved to re-examine his life in a new way. The workshop also allowed him a space to genuinely feel proud about his background and history. Now he works with his principal and teachers to run anti-racism workshops in which he shares his personal experience of growing up as a South Asian–Canadian in order to help others understand the effects of systemic bias and racism. And he now asks people to call him Jamshid.

Jamshid isn't alone in his realizations. Many people's lives have changed after these workshops, proving to me that culturally diverse stories and spaces where people can talk openly about their implications are profoundly important.

The person this storytelling probably affected the most, however, was me. *The Brown Book* project not only helped me make sense of who I was and where I came from but also firmly grounded my identity in Canada. Trying to imagine settling down anywhere other than Toronto became nearly impossible. This place was home. By exploring my South Asian roots I felt a profound sense of attachment and responsibility towards Canada. The two parts of my identity and history seemed to truly connect to each other for the first time.

To date more than three thousand copies of *The Brown Book* have been distributed, both nationally and internationally. Hundreds of educators have been trained in a unique *Brown Book* methodology that demonstrates how storytelling can be used to combat racism. In 2002 the Elementary Teachers' Federation of Ontario honoured *The Brown Book* project with the Anti-Bias Curriculum Development Award.

By the time I received the award I'd been an educator and community organizer for close to a decade both in Canada and abroad. Among other projects, I had worked in rain forests in Costa Rica, spearheaded political and economic literacy workshops for low-income communities, helped organize a variety of political and social events around Toronto, and put in countless volunteer hours for a number of community-based organizations. I thought that I had carved myself a fulfilling role in my community. But my outlook started to change.

A few weeks immediately following 9/11 I was sitting in a planning meeting for an event in the city to promote peace, justice, and understanding and watched as a group of activists and anti-racist advocates bickered and sniped at one another as they tried to decide what approach to take for the event given that a tragedy of immense magnitude had just occurred. The environment in the room was sharply political, divided, and terribly unfriendly—surprising, considering that these people supposedly held a common vision for the world. Instead of engaging in the argument, I began to detach from the situation.

Again and again, I had this experience. I was distracted, had trouble paying attention, and felt generally tired and irritated. This detachment also occurred in my personal life: I always managed to prioritize my work and the needs of strangers ahead of time with my loved ones, who began to wonder why I wasn't around and why I was always so exhausted. My life was in disarray. I felt resentful about giving so much of my time to the outside world and began to question what I was doing and why. I hit burnout and walked away from community organizing and activism.

I spent the next year reflecting on my life and getting counselling support, and I discovered a few things about myself. First, I'd been really angry at injustice in the world for a long time, and I realized this approach could only be a short-term strategy. There's a place for anger, but it can't be maintained forever—it's a tricky dance to keep that anger from becoming despair, self-righteousness, and isolation. Second, I became aware of certain destructive patterns in my life. For example, when my personal life was in turmoil, I always threw myself harder into organizing community programs and events. Rather than deal with my internal issues, I always sought to control and change my external environment.

I also learned some new skills, like finding peace by spending time in quietness and solitude, something I couldn't do before. I found myself not wanting to hang out in the same social scenes or keep in touch with the same number of people. I realized that I had a choice in how busy I was—that the world would continue to turn if I said no to people in my life and declined to participate in some community events. I learned to prioritize the various facets of my life a little better and block out the voices that seemed constantly to demand my attention. This downtime allowed new ideas, desires, and directions to emerge.

122

I realized that I needed projects that nurture me personally and allow me to be more creative. The performer in me started to speak, and before I knew it, I'd completed a year's worth of acting and improv classes. This new creative outlet became so compelling that I took an unpaid leave of absence from full-time teaching in 2003 to learn how to make films at

Ryerson University. I've completed my first independent film, *Andy in the City*, which was shot in December of 2004. It's a dramatic film about a young South Asian–Canadian named Anand who has to come to terms with his identity and his role in the family when his older brother, Raj—the pillar of support for everyone around him—has a breakdown and abandons the family. This film allowed me to explore the concepts of sacrifice and personal boundaries, patterns in family relationships, and the challenges of growing up in a society that sees you as an outsider.

Theatre and film are an exciting new direction for me. I feel that my politics, my perspectives on justice, and my passion for storytelling get to be expressed in new ways. As a diversity and leadership consultant now, I still conduct anti-racism workshops and raise awareness about racial issues for educators, students, and school board administrations—it's important and necessary work. I'm learning, however, to balance my internal personal needs with the demands of an external world that can be beautiful and kind as often as it's brutal and horrifying—this struggle to maintain equilibrium allows me to feel gratitude and not just despair, hope and not just anger.

After I published *The Brown Book*, I thought I had landed and found a sense of home. I realize now that it was simply one step in the right direction. The project was significant in that it allowed me to find my place in the Canadian society. My emotional burnout, however, made me realize that I had a much longer journey to travel: I had to find a sense of home within myself. And so, I continue exploring who I am, what I want, and where I'm supposed to be in order to understand my place in the world.

I am uncertain where this spiritual journey will lead, but I am committed to following it. By learning to listen to that small voice inside myself, I have found a deeper sense of peace, compassion, and gratitude than I have ever known. Don't get me wrong—there are still struggles and difficult days; it's just that I now find it easier to deal with the darkness and move past it. For now, I am in a pretty good place.

Salaam.

■ ■ ■ ■ ■

SHAKIL CHOUDHURY is co-founder of Anima Leadership (www. animaleadership.com), a consulting and training organization that specializes in leadership, diversity, and gender issues. He is part of a dynamic team of award-winning Canadian educators who have created powerful, cutting-edge leadership programs integrating emotional intelligence research with equity education and conflict  resolution skills. His innovative work has taken him to Europe, to the United States, to Latin America, and across Canada. Shakil is also writing a screenplay for his next film.

"AH. SO WE ARE ALL THE SAME": REFLECTIONS ON HUMAN DEVELOPMENT AND ATTITUDES IN ACTIVISM

Chris Richards

I SPENT MY TWENTY-THIRD birthday hunting for spare parts in Suame, a community of welders, mechanics, machinists, and other artisans in the city of Kumasi, Ghana, in West Africa. After haggling with shopkeepers all day I finally found the last part I needed. Anxious to get home, I made my way towards the main road, feeling the first drops of rain on the back of my neck. Looking up at the horizon spotted with TV antennas, I watched the sky quickly grey and darken. There was a strong, cold breeze, and then suddenly the rain came crashing down. I hid in a shop nearby and watched the gravel roads quickly become canals, directing water downhill to some unknown river of sewage and waste passing through the city. Boards that ten minutes ago looked to be strewn throughout the road in the oddest locations revealed themselves to be carefully laid bridges. Marvelling at this Venice in Africa, I glanced at my watch and realized I was going to be late again.

I was living with the Larbi family in Kumasi and knew they were planning a birthday feast for me that night. The cost to send me overseas as a volunteer with Engineers Without Borders (EWB) for four months is more than a local engineer would make in a year, and I knew that for my placement to be justified, I had to think of it as much more than just a chance to see and experience Africa. Working long hours caused me to be late for supper many nights, and as I thought of my host family waiting for me, I decided this night couldn't be one of them. I took a deep breath, filled my backpack with nuts, bolts, pulleys, belts, and pieces of sheet metal, and walked out into the pounding rain. It wasn't long, however, before I was forced to seek shelter under the overhang of a rusty metal roof.

The sun had already set, and the only light came from poorly spaced, crooked street lamps, making it hard to see through the falling water. Debating whether to venture out again, I watched as two small, naked, jet-black boys ran past me. One balanced a plastic bucket on his head, and he proceeded to use it to collect falling water from a bowed tin roof. The bucket filled quickly, and he began to weave his way down the road as the smaller boy gave chase, struggling in the slippery mud to keep up. It struck me that I am an anomaly on this earth. I belong to the minority of people with a life of abundance and privilege. Born a white Canadian male, my drinking water is safe. I have access to health care. My rights are protected. My voice is heard.

In Ghana I worked for a local non-governmental organization originally known as the Kumasi Institute for Technology and the Environment, but now simply called KITE. KITE's work includes supporting Ghanaian entrepreneurs, and the organization has a working partnership with Engineers Without Borders. My main task for that summer was to evaluate and support a food processing business KITE created in a rural village called Yaakrom.

The United Nations Development Programme originally developed the idea of these businesses in Mali, and KITE had been contracted to begin expanding them into Ghana. The business, called a multi-functional platform, used a diesel engine to power food processing machines. These machines were used throughout the country, but the business was unique in several ways; for example, an alternator ran off the flywheel of the diesel engine and charged batteries while the food processors either shredded or milled food brought in by a farmer. The added feature of the alternator increased earnings significantly with little additional fuel cost or operator time. KITE selected as their entrepreneurs for this pilot project Akua Fukuor and her husband, Peter Kwaku (I called him P.K.), two of the hardest working people I've ever met.

For many years the pair had operated a business in which they processed food by hand with the support of their extended family. It was this experience and their obvious work ethic that singled them out as ideal entrepreneurs for the pilot project. Their first business revolved around processing, cooking, and selling cassava, a large root vegetable similar to a yam or a very large potato. In a typical day Akua would wake before the sun rose at 6:00 AM to leave for her cassava farm and wouldn't return until after the sun had fallen at 6:00 PM. Because of a shoulder injury, P.K. was unable to farm, but he helped peel and grate the cassava, and, being a retired teacher, his education also enabled him to keep detailed records of their accounts.

One of the steps in processing cassava is to grate it until it looks like fibrous mashed potatoes. In Ghana women typically grate cassava by hand using a piece of tin with holes punched into it with a nail. Processing food by hand is arduous and time consuming. We hoped that mechanizing the process would free up time for women to earn more money for the family. Reducing the workload for the women in the community could also decrease the need for their daughters to help at home and allow more girls to attend school regularly. Once Akua and P.K. became entrepreneurs for the project they were able to use the machines to expand their business and increase the food processing services they could offer, including battery charging and mechanical grinding of cassava and corn.

This project was very business focused, and both EWB and KITE encouraged the entrepreneurs to work towards owning the technology and to be accountable to the people who gave them support and assistance. Before the food processing machines arrived KITE required Akua and P.K. to make an initial investment in their business by constructing the building that would house the machines. KITE then delivered and installed the machines and transferred ownership to Akua with the understanding that she would pay for them over time with the profits she and P.K. generated. KITE financed the project and also offered Akua a significantly reduced interest rate for her payments on the capital cost of the equipment (at the time interest in Ghana was 35 per cent). In turn, Akua and P.K. were responsible for keeping well-recorded accounts and making regular payments to KITE.

When I first arrived in Akua and P.K.'s village the machines had already been installed for about three months, and I could immediately see how well they operated the business as a team. Each day she collected a wagonload of cassava from the farm while P.K. ground corn and cassava that other local farmers brought to him. The machines greatly increased the amount of food the villagers could process, allowing them to sell and store more of their crops. In the region surrounding

Yaakrom there is an abundance of cassava, but it spoils quickly and much of the crop is wasted. Processing allows for longer storage periods and sales to markets in other regions of the country where demand may be higher. It was inspiring for me to work with P.K. and Akua as they expanded their business and managed new challenges and opportunities. My work in Ghana convinced me that supporting entrepreneurs can be an excellent way to promote human development.

There were four of us working on the project, three of us EWB volunteers from Canada—Kelsey Chegus from Edmonton, Mike Quinn from Calgary, and me. The fourth, Charles Agboada, had recently graduated from mechanical engineering at one of Ghana's universities. Each of the Canadian volunteers had a personal exit strategy, ensuring that by the time we left, the project would have no need for our presence. Of my four months in Ghana, I spent the first two working myself into a job and the last two working myself out. Our relationship with Charles was crucial to working ourselves out of a job in this way. Had Charles or another Ghanaian not worked beside us throughout the summer I wouldn't have felt comfortable contributing to the project, because I believe that although foreign development workers can have a great positive impact, development must be driven primarily by local leaders. We knew that Charles and the KITE staff would be the ones continuing the project long after we returned to Canada.

Kelsey, Mike, and I had many conversations with Charles that stretched late into the night. At first Charles didn't believe me when I told him that we had many homeless people in Canada. Images of white people in poverty don't reach that region of the world nearly as much as images depicting them as rich, powerful, and privileged. As the summer passed we talked about the equality of women, religion, human rights, alternative approaches towards our project, and the differences between Canada and Ghana. I talked a lot about Canada's diversity, and he leaned forward with interest when I spoke about Canada's First Nations people. But as I began to explain their history and situation to him I stopped myself, realizing I was completely ignorant about the subject and that the little I knew came from negative stereotypes and one-sided stories I'd heard from the media, my friends, and many others I had listened to as I was growing up. One of the biggest realizations of my journey to Ghana was just how much I needed to unlearn.

These late-night discussions changed my life, particularly the ones in which Charles spoke of religion, spirituality, and his goals in life. He was in his mid-thirties, and the youthful twinkle in his eye put us all at ease. I'm confident that he could have found a higher-paying job close to his home in the city, but instead he committed himself to working on the road, travelling from village to village, striving to learn more about the challenges rural people faced and how KITE could do a better job of helping them. He was deeply committed to helping the people of Ghana prosper and work against poverty. Charles rarely spoke negatively about other people, he kept an open mind and was a patient listener, and he spoke honestly about his thoughts and emotions.

We had such a positive impact upon each other. Charles helped me become more aware of myself, Canada, and Ghana. While I was in Ghana I would sometimes overhear self-deprecating comments from local people, such as one man who commented upon seeing my digital camera that such a wonderful thing could never be made in Africa. It's very difficult to come to terms with living and working with people who sometimes don't believe in themselves; discovering this attitude in some of the people I met is partly why I'll never forget the night that

Charles said to me softly as we talked about poverty in Canada, "Ah. So we are all the same." What a profound realization for Charles, to know for the first time that he was equal to everyone else on earth. It was the first time that I had fully realized it myself as well. The concept of universal equality moved from the rhetoric I had heard to a reality I truly understood. We sat there for a moment in silence, both knowing we were just human and there was nothing special about me that wasn't also special about him.

Although working with EWB and KITE was a generally positive experience, the project suffered some complications. There were times when we EWB volunteers did not take enough care in choosing our words, and these missteps undermined and hindered Charles in his work. For example, when we first arrived in Ghana the price of a car battery was 500,000 cedis (about CAD$69) and for four months, we had been quoting that price to our local partners. By the end of the summer, however, the country's inflation rate of 12.5 per cent had driven the cost of a battery to 550,000 cedis (CAD$76). Charles was concerned that after we left he would have to quote this higher price to the people in the remote villages to which we had travelled whose trust we had spent the summer trying to build. Charles worried that because they had limited communication with the markets in the city, they might wonder if he had raised the price in order to pocket 50,000 cedis for himself.

Another problem that we encountered was that the ownership structure and contract negotiations KITE and EWB had designed created conflict between Akua, P.K., and members of their family that they employed. The contracts gave ownership of the machines to Akua and legally recognized the business as hers; she enjoyed this role as a strong, independent businesswoman. But the business relied on a constant supply of food from their farm, and Akua was first and foremost a farmer. At night she and P.K. worked together, but during they day she spent almost all of her time working in the fields, while P.K. managed the business. The original business structure had designated their young nephew Ofosu as the business's operator; thus, although in practice P.K. was Ofosu's boss, Ofosu outranked him on paper. P.K.'s important role in the business had not initially been recognized in the official documents, and we noticed that this oversight left him feeling slighted.

The situation was further complicated by the fact that we often treated P.K., rather than Akua, as the entrepreneur. P.K. managed the machines during the day, spoke English fluently, and was quite well educated. Akua, in contrast, was always working on the farm, spoke little English, and had only a minimal education. She was incredibly smart and a natural entrepreneur, but when it came to talking about the business we unconsciously dealt directly with P.K. and made her feel left out. We relied on P.K. to help her understand the accounting he was doing or the business strategies we were brainstorming with him. Thankfully, P.K. was very supportive of Akua and patient with the process. I think in many ways he was the best development worker of all of us, and if he hadn't had such a wonderful attitude, much more conflict could have arisen.

At the end of the summer the business in Yaakrom was not doing as well as we had expected, and in my final report I told KITE that the project might fail because the business did not have sufficient market access. I had also heard that the alternator was broken. KITE and new EWB volunteers continue to support the project in Ghana, but without investing time and thought into addressing issues such as market access or maintenance, the machines in Yaakrom could become more remnants of failed development projects.

WHEN I RETURNED to Canada I felt the urge to share what I'd learned in Ghana by giving presentations and writing articles for local journals and newspapers. I have done far more public speaking than writing, having given over two dozen presentations in the past two years—to high-school and university students, and at conferences, at church services, and to professional engineering societies—about the lessons that I learned while I was in Ghana and the challenges of development work. One article that I did get published in Saskatoon's local newspaper was written after the tsunami struck Southeast Asia on Boxing Day in 2004. In it I discussed the vulnerability of people in poverty and highlighted how many more people are in need of aid around the world. In response I received an email from a local resident who angrily accused me of looking for a way to feel morally superior and hectoring others for not doing enough. He summarized our philosophical differences, writing:

> And finally, the great collectivist wheeze, that "We" must reduce poverty. I have absolutely no moral or economic obligation to anyone else, so don't try to make me feel guilty because someone has less than I do. By all means, hold your tin cup high and proud and send every nickel you raise to anyone you care to send it to—just leave me out of it.

There's a sliver of truth in what he wrote. Eyes widen when I casually mention I lived in the "Dark Continent." It's easy to gain respect and feel proud after volunteering overseas, and upon returning home sometimes the fires of a person's ego can burn high. Every day volunteers from all over the globe go overseas and return a few weeks later feeling very good about themselves, often accomplishing little at the expense of a great deal of resources, or in the worst cases having done more damage than good. Sometimes I wonder about my own time in

Ghana and worry that I've taken more from the people than I have given them. And like the man who emailed me I've also come to grow weary of the angry activists—individuals who stand on soapboxes and condemn others, unable to understand how we ever came to be so terrible.

I answered his email asking, "If you were in a car accident tomorrow, would you expect a passing stranger to stop and help you? Is it acceptable for them to walk a little faster, locking their eyes on something they pretend to be interested in, ignoring all of the ugly things they saw that day?" I believe that for community to function we can't travel down a path of conscious ignorance and non-compassion. I've learned instead that it is important to become educated, stay positive, and take action. It's easy to become angry and cynical, and it's a challenge to accept that we can't do everything and that our contributions won't be perfect, but together it's possible to move the world in a positive direction.

It's with this mentality that, when I came back to Canada, I started Footprint Design—Engineering Towards Sustainability, a student group based out of the College of Engineering at the University of Saskatchewan. I perceived a need within the college for an organization that addressed environmental issues, and I found many students eager to help me. Footprint's goal is to provide opportunities for critical learning and thinking about how best to work towards sustainability. The group now has a student executive that has organized two public forums covering topics including wind power, biodiesel, waste management, energy-efficient homes, and the ecological perspective of First Nations people, in addition to coordinating tours for students to see examples of local environmental leadership in industry and the community. Our tours have included the Eco-Centre in Craik, Saskatchewan, which uses straw bales for its insulation, and a biogas plant in Cudworth, Saskatchewan. The plant is owned by Clear-Green Environmental Inc., a company that extracts biogas and nutrients from organic waste such as hog manure.

WHEN I FINALLY made it home for my birthday supper with my family that night I was drenched and late again. The rain had finally stopped, and I sat with a tired sigh on the lawn chair in my family's compound. But my spirits brightened when my sisters and mother came rushing out of the house both to tease me for being late and to reheat supper. The Larbis taught me that to be without borders is to care for all people, to accept anyone into your family as if they were your own, just like they did with me.

One of the greatest gifts of my experience in Ghana was having my worldview repeatedly shattered. I can never again look at a world map with the eyes I had before my time in Africa. Now I see the twenty million people in the country labelled Ghana; before there was nothing. I have glimpsed the incredible diversity and vastness of humanity, and I feel both incredibly powerful and incredibly small.

The complexity of how best to fulfill EWB's mission to promote human development often leaves me feeling impotent. I remain filled with hope, however, and I'm excited to finish my master's degree and volunteer overseas again for EWB. My summer in Ghana would never have been as enriching without the training I received from EWB, and I want to work for them again because I believe in their attitude towards development—it's one of humility, respect, and equality in a framework of co-operative partnerships. They are also committed to continually questioning the status quo, learning, and striving to be better. My work with both EWB and Footprint

Design has convinced me that I have the power to make a difference. But I've also learned that when we work for change it is in the face of incredible complexity, and we cannot expect to control or understand every detail. I believe, then, that it is our attitudes that determine our course and our final destination.

■ ■ ■ ■ ■

CHRIS RICHARDS spent four months in Ghana with Engineers Without Borders (www.ewb.ca) then returned to his home in Saskatoon, Saskatchewan, where he is currently a master's student in mechanical engineering. Chris founded Footprint Design (www.footprintdesign. usask.ca) at the University of Saskatchewan in 2004, an innovative organization focused on sustainable engineering design. He now focuses on using his experience with EWB and Footprint's unique

approach to engineering to educate students about sustainability and to provide them with opportunities to think critically about Canada's role in the world. He would like to dedicate this piece to Peter "P.K." Kwaku, who died in November 2005 due, it is believed, to tuberculosis. Medicines that treat TB are free in Canada.

DUB POETICS AND
PERSONAL POLITICS

d'bi.young.anitafrika
edited by devin francis

POETRY IS THE way we help give name to the nameless so it
can be thought —audre lorde

the personal is political
mama said *a storyteller is a gate-keeper.* in the tradition of dub
poetry (a legacy descended from the afrikan griots) i am a
keeper of gates and herstories. the dub poet speaks in the people's language, using music and rhythm, gesture and expression to tell the story and connect with the audience. this
connection with the audience is symbolic of the poet's personal commitment to community: being both responsible for
and accountable to them. this commitment is woven into dub's
aesthetics and politics. the poet inhabits and reclaims trou-
bled spaces, making the community aware of its capacity for
change and love. this *love* is the genesis of revolushun; and is

simultaneously micro- and macrocosmic, transforming the personal and romantic into the political and social.

i believe that politics is a product of experience, not just the imposed experiences of reality but the interpreted reality of understanding and choice. dub asks that the storyteller be in a consistent process of honest and integritous self-analysis and critique in order to do the same as a storyteller within the community. dub tradition has shaped and embellished my socio-cultural and political hybridism as a womban raised in both jamaica and canada. dub allows me to draw new understandings from old experiences. it allows me to constantly reinvestigate the philosophies that inform my art. my personal realities and political convictions are closely intertwined; so much so that it is difficult to say exactly where one ends and the other begins.

jump out of the frying pan and jump inna fyah
the seventies, eighties, and early nineties—the years of my childhood and adolescence—were very turbulent times in jamaica. england, weakened by the expenditures of the second world war, could no longer hold on to its colonies. jamaica won its independence in 1962. jamaica, like many other former colonies, was left with an underdeveloped economy unable to sustain itself or feed its people. in the wake of the cuban missile crisis and the tensions of the cold war, america became acutely aware of the geopolitical significance of the caribbean. and regularly intervened in the affairs of newly independent caribbean states.

during the first rule of michael manley, jamaica flirted with socialism—making overtures to the soviet union and forging alliances with castro's cuba. however, american interventionism complicated jamaica's development of a stable socio-economic and political structure. the country spun into insolvency on the *neo-colonial hamster's wheel* of indebtedness. the IMF and world bank—agents of elite U.S. interests—lent money, conditionally. structural adjustment programs diverted the nation's resources from health and education to service the interest on debts; and to make jamaica attractive to foreign investment and ownership, the nation's currency was devalued.

the 1980 elections between the long-standing *people's national party* and the american-supported *jamaica labour party* was the bloodiest the country had ever experienced. the election of seaga and america's invasion of grenada ended all hopes of jamaica joining cuba in its socialist groundation. the society crashed into the harsh realities of extreme poverty. jamaicans were sold the *american dream* and with it, the tools for its subliminal and forced implementation: drugs, weapons, and ammunition. these goods were purchased with the blood of ghetto youths, as jamaica simmered, then exploded, with the anger of the oppressed.

this jamaica was the backdrop of my childhood. this jamaica midwifed the birth of dub poetry.

how the body remembers
i am a very angry person. i cannot deny my anger. it has been very important in my work as an artist. i have grown to love and respect my anger, because it is a potent source of energy; this energy, when channelled from a place of love, is a powerful motivational tool for social change. it is righteous anger at the numerous legacies of injustice left by the british that was the prime inspirational tool for early dub poets who chanted down racism, shadeism, classism, and sexism, among other issues in the late seventies, early eighties.

anger *is* the potential for change. it is important in the healing process. it shows us which parts hurt; which parts of ourselves need to be reclaimed. from this place of righteous anger, we claim our body (the most intimate space of oppression) as a site of expression, pleasure, and resistance. watching the dub poets as i grew up, i learned that one of the greatest tools of storytelling is allowing the body to feel.

language is an attempt to name how we feel. paper poetry is often different from the language that lives in people's mouths. the jamaican nation language is a survival tongue that comes out of the belly of west afrika, dressed up in english vocabulary, grammar, and syntax with splinterings of awarak and carib, french and dutch talk; it is by its very nature a site of resistance. language is essential in dub because the poet speaks the language of the people. british literature was the only valuable poetry studied in primary, secondary, and post-secondary institutions in jamaica. this literature was possessed with parallels equating blackness with evil and whiteness with good, blackness with stupidity and whiteness with intelligence, blackness with deceit and whiteness with honesty, et cetera. early dub poets, while reading chaucer, shakespeare, and wordsworth, knew that a part of their battle against imperialism meant interrogating the linguistic oppression meted out by the british. they wrote poetry that everyday working-class jamaicans could identify with because it sounded like a street-corner conversation one was having with a friend. in the oral tradition, language inhabits the body; therefore, in telling a story it must live within you.

naming yourself

i was surrounded by poets growing up—everyday people who might not have put pen to paper or recited for an audience, but their bodies, faces, voices spoke the rhythms and rawness of their lives and expressed their feelings, thoughts, and disappointments in powerful and distinct ways. they were more than just poets; storytelling resided in their spirits.

these everyday stories found their way into the music i grew
up listening to: *dancehall, hiphop,* and *reggae.* the lyrics chronicled the violence and anger of ghetto life as well as romantic
love, religion, and sex. a small percentage of the music had a
political analysis; however, it was dub that put this violence
and anger within a socio-political framework, linking it to
decisions that were being made by people who didn't live in
our communities.

i was also blessed by the influence of dub practitioners
such as anita stewart (my mother), mikey smith, jean binta
breeze, cherry natural, oku onuora, and linton kwesi johnson.
these mentors were village elders (not because they were old—
they were mostly in their early twenties when they began—
but because they were wise) who harnessed the poetic energy
of the people, refined it, and organized it under a revolution-
ary anti-oppressive politic. they used language, political con-
tent, music, and performance—the four main elements of the
dub tradition, to provoke, politicize, and ultimately to exor-
cise and heal.

i was instantly attracted to that power, watching my mother
perform when i was four years old. at thirteen, i began to call
myself a dub poet. i wrote twelve or thirteen poems, recorded
them, and sent them to my mother who had been living in canada since the previous year. i would join her in a couple years,
inevitably undergoing the redefining madness of culture shock.

gawn to foreign
coming to canada at age fifteen was traumatic: culture shock,
racism, the unbelievable and merciless cold. once you get past
these, questions around identity, belonging, and assimilation
plague you like horseflies. i hid behind make-up and a linguistic chameleon-like ability to simulate the canadian accent. i
had had a lot of practice in jamaica on the art of changing one's

identity. being from a ghetto community and attending campion college (an upper-middle-class/upper-class school), where the wealthy and privileged sent their children, facilitated a hybridism of *identity a* at home and *identities b, c,* or *d* at school depending on who i needed to be on that day. my experience in both home and school spaces was alienating at best and taught me first-hand about the opportunism of oppression.

interestingly enough, however, when i came to canada i quickly began to claim my conflicted upbringing in jamaica as home, clinging to my jamaican-ness as my primary place of identification. it took me twelve years before i began referring to myself as jamaican-canadian: a hybrid.

as i became older and more exposed to the works of dub poets such as ahdri zhina mandiela, afua cooper, lillian allen, and the feminist theory of bell hooks, audre lorde, and tracy chapman, the multiplicity of my identity began to shard itself like broken pieces of glass, stabbing at my conditioned bigotries and creating internalized polarities. these questions regarding queerness versus homophobia, working class versus privileged, xenophobia versus recognizing-everyone-as-an-immigrant-on-first-nations-territory, became the macrocosms to my microconcerns about attractiveness, intelligence, talent, and my future. always our different selves collide—sometimes destructively and other times growingly. new parts of ourselves become apparent to us. during the first four years of being in canada new parts of myself burst forth as i grew—each part making me more aware of the others.

142

poetic identity
i am an able-bodied, black, working-class, afro-jamaican-canadian womban, queer, loving womben and men, dub poet, actor, playwright, and single mother of a young black boy,

partnering with a black man, living in toronto, canada, in the post-millennial era. that's a lot to integrate. dub tradition has guided me into this heterogeneity of herstory, history, and heritage; compelling me to claim all these parts of myself in resistance and struggle.

i've lived all over the place, including france, corsica, new york, cuba, and montreal. those were wonderful and enriching experiences that showed me a world perspective you sometimes don't get when you always live in one place. but it is incredible to live and work in toronto, this *meeting place* as they say. here, i too have become a meeting place; my spoken language, a meeting place. my body and mind and spirit, a crossroads of realities. divisions. disjunctures. intersections. we all live contradictions. none of us is really any one thing. storytelling helps me to move towards better integration of these multi-selves; allowing me to find freedom in the spaces in between.

telling stories from this place of multiplicity is my most valuable asset. it allows me to talk with people instead of at them. it allows me to implicate myself in the problems and suggest solutions.

responsibility and accountability

there is anger here. canada—like jamaica—is built on blood; first nations blood, afrikan blood, south- and east-asian blood, and the blood, sweat, and tears of working-class peoples. systemic injustice flourishes despite toronto's modernity and diversity; our bright and bubbling metropolis has a palpable anger—an anger that manifests itself very differently from the kinds that i grew up with—but anger nonetheless. home-grown like the domestic anger of inequality and imported like how i felt when i got here; the anger of the oppressed. it is through the experience of my colonized self that i am able to work and be in this place.

we have a material understanding of poverty—not having money or not having enough food. but poverty is economic domination. the oppressed, be it on the basis of race, gender, sexuality, or ability are always *poor*—our options limited by the actions of others. without the freedom and power to self-determine, our potential, or willingness to love and be loved, is greatly challenged. how can we express our complete human-ity in love-stunted environments?

my responsibility and accountability as a dub poet is to understand and address this issue. challenging the breadth and depth of oppression as it sophisticates and multiplies within this present canadian context is a part of my reinterpretation of dub tradition. i realized as i began taking the practice of dub poetry more seriously that i could not simply regurgitate the political analyses of pioneer dub—race and class exami-nation—but needed instead to transport the framework of dub to present-day socio-political concerns; using my art to enter silent spaces where pioneer dub would never have gone because it was a different time and place. some of my analyses around gender construction, sexuality, and homophobia have been met with strong resistance even within dub poetic spaces. however, i continue to negotiate some key tenets of the genre: provoke, challenge, and confront. i find solace in the fact that i am one of many people doing this kind of work, telling these kinds stories.

144

'da kink in my hair

i began playing the role of stacyanne in *'da kink in my hair* when i was twenty-two years old. i am now twenty-eight and preparing to go to england to share her story again; six years is a long time. this particular journey has taught me that the story is never the same. dub poetry says that a storyteller is always affected by his or her village; therefore, when the village changes, so does the storyteller.

i have told stacyanne's story to young black wombten, to old white wombten, to men and wombten of colour from all walks, to academics, to all kinds of working-class people. in each scenario the humanity of the story always takes precedence over the differences among the people witnessing it. in each telling stacyanne changes and grows and regresses, being held by her audience as she holds them; allowing whatever particular village to pour themselves into her. finding catharsis and healing. throughout this process i sit, watching the magic of reciprocity in full effect. storytelling in full effect.

'da kink made me a true believer.

watering our roots
i have a son, moon. he's the blessing i hoped for; the single spiritual force propelling me into the face of integrity. raising children can ground you in ways that usually take decades of experience. being responsible for another human being, helping to shape their thought patterns, influencing how they give and receive love, showing them how to take better care of mother earth, are all responsibilities i now know intimately. the theoretical approach to social change that i had for years finally concretized when moon came; a perfect place to practise the art of loving.

this new environment of mother and child highlighted | 145
behaviour patterns and emotional triggers within me that i thought were exorcised. i realized yet again that years of ingesting violence and hate don't just disappear simply because you want them to. change takes work. having moon sent me

back to the drawing board of dub, encouraging me to integrate this new/old knowledge of reconditioning abusive behaviour patterns; transforming violence into love.

i am challenged to find new ways to teach him about the broad spectrum of gender: allowing him room to develop and discover his manhood and humanity within a loving and encouraging environment; teaching him about positive and progressive ways to treat the people around him and disciplining him in firm yet loving ways when he experiments with not-so-loving behaviour.

i'm teaching him to appreciate stories and to be aware of their power. i take him everywhere with me; like my mother took me everywhere with her. babies are the best kind of observers, because they watch without judgment. his learning reminds me to keep learning as well. he reminds me that storytelling is a loving critique; a loving resistance. our griot tradition continues . . .

i dub poet d'bi.young

i
sometimes She-wind shifts her course
swirls softly about my head
making me remember
dub plates dancing on black vinyl
a slow rub-a-dub
pounding the pressures
of a people transferred
dub/poetry birthing herself through a canal
of concrete jungle/chaos and/ community
the griot in americas

ii
dis/covering roots dawtah
a push 'gainst di parametah
of a box-like strukchah
envisioning a more circular form
womb/and a dub ovah di version side a di 33 or di 45
popular reggae vibez
when we siddung pon street cornah
a watch di yout dem bout yah
a chant dung babylon
complex
while a real/lize
fi tear dung
yuh mus build up
and climb inward
di cycle is a circle
weh mus continue

iii
i am a poet
whose heart in balance with the wind
stands still
i am
one
i am many
herstories
alone
one bridge whose links hang
worn
i am tomorrow's forgotten yesterday
a programmed amnesia
a dys/functional

re/invention of the wheel
change is a hela/cycle
changing remaining the same
how will the scroll keepers grow
how will i grow
how will you grow

my son
how will you grow

■ ■ ■ ■ ■

D'BI.YOUNG.ANITAFRIKA (www.dbiyoung.net) is a Jamaican-Canadian dub poet, actor, and playwright who has performed throughout Canada, the Caribbean, Latin America, and Europe. She has produced four dub poetry albums and is currently working on her fifth, entitled *ky.ky.* Her first book of poetry, *art on black,* was

published by Women's Press, and her first one-woman play *blood.claat* was published by Playwrights Canada Press as a bilingual English-Spanish edition, both in 2006. d'bi.young is a resident artist at Soulpepper Academy and is currently developing two new plays: *androgyne* and *chronicles in dub.* She resides in Toronto with her son, Moon.

ON AUTHORITY
AND ACTIVISM

Robin Rix

ASK AN ACTIVIST about authority, and you might hear it described as something to be fought, subverted, and even overthrown. Conversely, ask an authority figure about activism, and you might hear it described as reckless, irresponsible, and destructive. Images of demonstrators being tear-gassed or beaten by riot police, protestors yelling at politicians and businesspeople, and out-of-touch leaders making decisions without regard to the social consequences of their actions have all contributed to mutual suspicion and even hostility between the two sides.

I want to challenge this dualism. Activism and authority don't need to be viewed as opposites. My own experiences—as an activist who recognizes the importance of authority—have led me to believe not only that activists can wield authority in ways that further their aims but that authority can also be activist in nature.

NOTES FROM CANADA'S YOUNG ACTIVISTS

In July 1997 I was a skinny nineteen-year-old working in Finland for the summer. I was working with a tiny grassroots organization to improve public acceptance of refugees. I took trains, boats, and buses as I criss-crossed the country giving presentations about where Finland's refugees came from, how many of them there were, where they were settling, and so on. This job took me to a "rock against racism" music festival in the little country town of Mariehamn, on an island off the southwest coast of Finland, where I would staff a booth and talk about refugees to passersby.

I helped the organizing team set up the festival. The main attraction was a local rock band playing on a makeshift stage. The audience would sit on logs, on tree stumps, and on the grass. Booths would ring the back of the audience—a Chinese restaurant offered plates of spring rolls and dumplings, an Indian clothing store set out saris and sarongs, and I had some glossy United Nations pamphlets about refugees. We expected around two hundred people.

About an hour before the concert one of the team members rushed up to the concert site. He'd heard on the radio that a group of neo-Nazis was scheduled to hold a meeting nearby, and he warned us that they might decide to crash our party. We looked nervously around at each other. We weren't strong enough to fend off a horde of potentially violent fanatics. Some members of the team suggested rescheduling the festival or shutting it down entirely.

Then one of the older and quieter guys spoke up. He said shutting down the event would send precisely the wrong message. Of course, he said, we should take sensible precautions, like alerting the police and having an emergency plan in place, but fear and hate should never be allowed to overpower what was right. We shouldn't let the neo-Nazis silence us, he added.

We all looked at one another and, slowly, started to nod. We posted lookout points around the concert, made sure that we had the appropriate emergency phone numbers on hand, and designated a couple of the bigger guys as security at the entrance.

The festival went ahead. The band played its sets, the spectators ate spring rolls and tried on sarongs, and I gave away all my pamphlets. The neo-Nazis, thankfully, never showed up. And it was the personal authority of that one man, quiet but confident, that strengthened the resolve of the rest of us not to buckle to intimidation and hate.

Almost three years later, as a graduate student in England, I held a part-time job helping to lead a youth group of male refugees and asylum-seekers who'd fled the Taliban in Afghanistan. One of them had escaped from captivity. He was missing his eyes.

Far away from the dreaming spires and grassy meadows that Oxford is known for, we met in a smoky old community centre amid housing projects and ramshackle Victorian laneways. It was hard trying to give these young men hope when they had little money, few prospects, and no one but each other.

I followed the lead of my colleague. Unconventional and sassy, she mesmerized the group with stories about having a child when she was fourteen years old, with jokes, and with tips on everything from personal safety to places to meet women in Oxford. Her easygoing and gentle nature relaxed everyone, including me, and helped facilitate conversations about Afghanistan, England, and life as a refugee. And it was the personal authority of my colleague who helped to bring hope and laughter where one might expect neither to exist.

After two years at Oxford I returned to Toronto and went to law school. During my first two years there, I served as a residence don in one of the undergraduate colleges—a job that required me to be a disciplinarian as well as a mentor.

I remember a great deal from those two years: breaking up fights, helping to supervise parties, caring for the occasional person who drank too much on a Saturday night, and offering advice about everything from academic to personal to financial issues.

My most vivid memory from that period, however, is kneeling next to a single bed in a dorm room and listening to a student away from home for the first time tell me that he was depressed and thinking about killing himself. I sat with him for more than an hour, talking with him and asking him questions, before confirming that he'd be all right for the next little while and helping him make an appointment with a professional counsellor.

I heard a few years later that he was doing well—having spent some time travelling, sorting out his personal problems, and reconnecting with his family and friends—and I smiled. It had been my personal authority as a role model and mentor that supported this person through a difficult period in his life.

In each of these experiences I learned a bit more about the power of personal authority, and I saw how people in authority can do good things. With the right phrase at the right time they can spur others to act for positive change, and they can use their positions to help people overcome tough external circumstances or battle their inner demons. These positions of authority aren't necessarily in governments or large organizations; they can also exist on a smaller scale amid the interactions of everyday life.

Many activists, however, see assuming authority as an act of selling out. I would argue that authority is only detrimental if it is wielded in thoughtless or evil ways. Rather than fighting authority, wouldn't it more productive for activists to teach people in authority how to use it more effectively, or even to assume positions of authority themselves?

I've tried to adopt this strategy of developing leadership skills for my own activism, and my education, both formal and informal, has supported me in this pursuit. It helped, I think, that my life has generally been conducive to learning. Thanks to my parents, who immigrated to Canada with nothing more than two crates of belongings, a dog, and the clothes on their backs, my childhood in Toronto was a relatively normal one in which I went to school regularly, played street hockey, and was more than adequately housed, fed, and loved. I went to the local elementary school and then to high school in The Annex, one of those trendy quasi-bohemian neighbourhoods with funky cafés and small boutiques that exist in any city over a certain size.

My schooling taught me to think critically, encouraged me to analyze issues from different angles, and introduced me to other people who held strong opinions about the same issues that I was interested in, including law, politics, and literature. But I have also taken advantage of the education that takes place outside the classroom: I became involved in student associations, including student governments and newspapers. I took jobs not so much for the money but for what I could learn from them. I tried to expose myself as much as I could to new ideas, new cultures, and new people, through pan-Canadian conferences and second-language immersion programs.

During my years at law school I went further afield and actively sought internships at human rights organizations in Nunavut and Ghana. In Nunavut I researched the inclusion of certain provisions relating to the proposed territorial human rights act, which aimed to provide an integrated approach to liberal democratic rights and the concept of "Inuit Qaujima-jatuqanginnut," translated approximately as "the Inuit way of doing things, whether past, present, or future." In Ghana I researched the legal status of people living with HIV and AIDS with respect to housing, health care, and employment rights, in partnership with non-governmental organizations from Ghana and Canada. Both internships developed my understanding of the importance of policy development and the far-reaching effects that public policies—and the people who develop them—have on people's lives. Subsequently, I completed my legal training at a firm with some great people, finally qualifying as a lawyer in July 2005, and immediately afterwards accepted a fellowship to work on projects in human rights and public policy in India and Canada, including research assignments on youth voter turnout and civic engagement.

These experiences showed me that activism isn't only about agitating for social change, raising awareness, leading protests, and shouting slogans. Activism is also about time, patience, and experience. It's about keeping your eyes open, exposing yourself to the full and free marketplace of ideas and people, developing as a person, and preparing yourself for the day when you find yourself, whether by choice or by chance, in a position of wielding personal authority.

If, in the future, I find myself in a position of authority, I hope to use it for the same activist goals that I value: asking people to question their assumptions, bringing hope to people in challenging circumstances, or helping people individually through difficult periods in their lives. Activism and authority aren't opposites—they are instead the opposite of opposites: they depend on each other. Activism without authority can often be futile, and authority without activism can often lack meaning.

154

ROBIN RIX received his undergraduate and law degrees from the University of Toronto and his graduate degree in political science from Oxford University. He qualified as a lawyer in 2005 and now works in the commodity derivatives and emissions trading practice group of Clifford Chance LLP in London, England. In 2002 he won the nationwide As Prime Minister essay prize (www.asprimeminister.com) sponsored by the Magna Foundation. He has worked on human rights projects in Finland, Ghana, and India, and he has been a member of Canada25 (www.canada25.com) for the past four years.

WATERSHED MOMENTS
OF A MÉTIS MENTOR

Kris Frederickson ■ ■
                    ■

I GREW UP IN rural Manitoba in a loving family of four. My father, a cabinetmaker, started his own business after working for somebody else for years. He didn't have a formal education—hell, he didn't even have a high-school diploma. What he did have were the necessary skills and business savvy to make his product the best it could be. His small, single-person company has been constantly busy for the last twenty-three years, and he's widely regarded as one of the best cabinetmakers in the area. From my perspective, this success is an astounding accomplishment for the middle boy of a six-child, blue-collar Métis and Icelandic family in rural Manitoba. I've learned a lot from my father's achievements, and I think I've inherited some of his entrepreneurial spirit, which has driven me to seek out opportunities to meet unfulfilled needs.

From my mother, I've learned that the vulnerable and less fortunate need partnership and support while they get on their feet. She is a pure and whole-hearted political and social activist and constantly raises her voice in defence of the disenfranchised. She will participate in anything from women's rights protests to anti-war demonstrations. She is a long-running school trustee in our community, and she ran in three provincial elections as a representative for the New Democrats in a former Conservative stronghold. She taught me that despite the odds, a person can achieve success through dedication and hard work. Through our many discussions she instilled in me the importance of questioning the status quo and striving for something better. We may have had different ideas about how to help people, but we've always agreed on the need. We still have some healthy and fiery debates on the role of government in economic development, education, and Canadian foreign policy.

My parents' expectations for me were high but not unrealistic. My love for them drove me to want to succeed. (Only later in life did I recognize the inherent satisfaction that comes from doing one's best.) As a graduate of engineering at the University of Manitoba, I was the first of my father's large family to receive a university degree. Like my parents, I strongly believe that lifelong education, formal and informal, is essential to reaching one's full potential.

This belief motivated me, as one of a handful of Métis engineers in Canada, to mentor Aboriginal youth. Christine Pierre, the Aboriginal Recruitment Officer at the University of Manitoba, hired me as a member of the Aboriginal U-Crew, a group that spoke to high-school students to encourage them to attend university. Obviously, our intent was to persuade them to study at the University of Manitoba, but our overarching goal was to impress upon them the importance of post-secondary education to joining Canada's modern workforce.

From that original, intimidating classroom presentation my mentoring expanded to include speaking at conferences, trade fairs, and workshops, and I continued to mentor throughout my years at university. In 2003 I received a National Métis Youth Role Model Award for Career Advancement, an honour that brought with it a responsibility to counsel other Métis youth on their many available career options. During my work with them I promoted education and careers in science and technology and tried to relay the advice and encouragement my own mentors have given me—to take responsibility for one's own actions, to persevere through adversity, and to gain wisdom patiently through one's experiences.

I still enjoy opportunities to speak to schools and professional associations in both Alberta and Manitoba. My audience has grown to include professional engineers and tradespeople, with whom I discuss such issues as Aboriginal inclusiveness and understanding in a Eurocentric society. I have participated on teams that have helped organizations, like the Association of Professional Engineers, Geologists, and Geophysicists of Alberta (APEGGA), establish their own Aboriginal inclusiveness policy and design events geared towards encouraging partnerships between Aboriginal and non-Aboriginal engineers.

I hope that by perpetuating understanding, acceptance, and encouragement, I can help play a part in undoing the effects of past paternalistic government policies. These policy outcomes, like the Indian Act, the spectre of residential schools, the forced removal of children from their homes and families, the banning of native languages, and the destruction of traditional lands and ways of life, spurred the cultural genocide of the First Nations of Canada. Still, despite every effort to destroy our various cultures, intentional or otherwise, and despite the many barriers to success the Aboriginal community faces—including poverty, racism, addictions, and health issues—our peoples are strong and have proven their resiliency. I believe that if I can spark imagination and inspiration in the youth I mentor, that spark will grow into a flame of enthusiasm and a drive to succeed. I hope to help Aboriginal youth strive for something great, make their world a little less intimidating, and broaden their perspective of what they can accomplish.

The people I've met through my mentoring have rewarded me with rich cultural experiences. Although I've always been keenly aware of my Métis heritage, I didn't grow up in a religious or even spiritual family. My father, being a tradesperson, values the concrete and practical: objects he can hold and make with his hands. Our family rarely discussed the supernatural and the spiritual, since these ideas didn't help put food on the table. Although this pragmatic approach may serve the entrepreneur well in matters of business, I've come to understand that for some, there is more to life.

Christine Pierre, former boss–turned–close friend, was the first to introduce me to a traditional sweat. I will never forget the experience in that Eagle lodge. The heat of the hot stones that hold the spirits of our grandmothers and grandfathers enveloped me in the pitch darkness. The medicines that hung close in the air at first constricted the throat but opened up both my lungs and mind to the warmth of Mother Earth. That first sweat was very personal, and it gave me clarity of purpose in my studies and reminded me to remain humble in the light of success.

I have since had the opportunity to attend several sweats both in Manitoba and in the Yukon. Each sweat encompassed a different teaching: one taught me to care for my community while remembering not to neglect myself; another taught me to reach out to people with whom I may be in conflict and try to resolve our differences through empathy and understanding.

Although every sweat was unique, the timing of each was always perfect.

From the teachings in the sweat lodge and discussions with Christine and Mike, her husband, I have developed a better appreciation for the powerful spiritual symbols of the medicine wheel, including the cyclical nature of life. The medicine wheel is divided into quadrants with each direction of the compass having its own power. The quadrants represent many key teachings. Most important to me is that they represent the mental, emotional, physical, and spiritual cornerstones of life. The medicine wheel reminds me that these cornerstones are closely interconnected and that life seeks an equilibrium I must strive to achieve. The quadrants of the medicine wheel also represent the four archetypal elements of the world. Air resides in the east while Earth lives in the south; Fire exists in the west and Water, the element to which I feel the most kinship, lies in the north.

I have always had a love of water. Some of my fondest memories of childhood are of fishing with my dad. We lived a short ride away from the Red and Assiniboine rivers and Lakes Manitoba and Winnipeg. But it wasn't until I went to Fort McMurray to work for Syncrude Canada as an engineering student that I began to see a different side to water. The Athabasca tar sands hold a great deal of oil, approximately 350 billion barrels' worth, and to extract this oil requires a lot of water. I found it difficult to reconcile the huge tailings ponds of polluted water with the pristine lakes meant for swimming and playing that were a staple of my youth. However, one mentor I had during my work term was an avid mountaineer, and I was fortunate enough to go rock climbing with him. He showed through his actions that he felt it was important to minimize one's ecofootprint and to clean up after oneself and others when given the opportunity—he often went out of his way to pick up stray pop bottles and deposit them in the recycling bin. His deep respect for the environment was contagious and belied his career in the oil industry. His seemingly paradoxical nature taught me that one's personal actions are the only thing over which one has control and that these actions can make a difference in spite of larger forces at work.

My interest in water-related issues continued to grow as I took my first engineering position helping to reclaim lands disturbed by tar sands mining. I saw how rainwater caused us grief as it eroded gullies in the sand hills we had made. This experience prompted me to go to Australia for a four-month stint at the National Centre for Engineering in Agriculture (NCEA). There I studied the effects of a particular tropical grass used to prevent stream bank erosion due to flash floods. The NCEA offices are in Toowoomba, Queensland, in an agricultural district known as the Darling Downs. This area west of Brisbane is semi-arid, and the people there have a heightened appreciation for water. They collect every last drop, and there are elaborate schemes to account for the water used by the communities and farmers in the region. Coming from a water-rich country like Canada, I found this experience eye-opening. I had been able to view water through three different lenses: as a source of recreation in Manitoba, a tool in commercial development in Alberta, and a necessity for life in Australia.

Upon returning from Australia I shifted my focus to water treatment when I performed an engineering scan of data collected by Indian and Northern Affairs Canada and discovered that over a third of water and sewage treatment systems in Aboriginal communities in Manitoba were vastly inadequate, potentially causing an environmental and health crisis affecting thousands of people. I took an immediate interest. "Here is a project worth spending my time on, because I can directly influence the community," I thought. I began pursuing a master's degree in biosystems engineering in an effort to find a technical answer to the crisis, and I ended up working on a system called a membrane bioreactor.

Traditional water treatment counts on gravity to pull large particles out of wastewater and bacterial sludge to biodegrade the water's organic components. A membrane bioreactor couples the power of bacteria with a membrane, which not only filters particulates from the water, but also stops the bacteria from escaping, allowing the biological reaction to occur in a smaller tank. My hope was that this system would allow remote Canadian communities to reduce their capital costs by building smaller plants. The system proved to produce very good water, but it had drawbacks that I had not anticipated: the membranes were expensive, and the system could be complicated to operate in a community that may not have the necessary trained personnel to maintain the reactor. I thus discovered during my master's research that new technology, however elaborate and well-intentioned, may not always be the best solution to engineering problems.

I have taken the knowledge, wisdom, and spirituality from my experiences, as well as from my family, mentors, and colleagues, to Alberta where I now work as a water management engineer for global energy producer Nexen Inc., a company some activists in environmental circles may deem the "bad guys." I am fully aware of how inconsistent and even hypo-

critical my career direction appears. However, I derive solace from the fact that I strive to effect environmentally sustainable change from within my organization. By working for Nexen, I have been given the opportunity to both learn about the oil industry and, by harnessing the entrepreneurial tools

I gleaned from my father and the drive for justice I acquired from my mother, communicate the ideas of sustainability to my co-workers. I am not so naive to believe that I can change the industry in a few days or even a few years, but through my personal actions I hope to display my passion for the environment and ultimately protect the water that I love, one drop at a time.

■ ■ ■ ■ ■

KRIS FREDERICKSON received his Master of Science degree from the University of Manitoba and is now a water management engineer with global oil and gas producer Nexen in Calgary. He is also the co-chair of 2335 (www.2335.ca), a United Way initiative focused on increasing civic engagement in the demographic of twenty-three- to thirty-five-year-olds. In 2004 Kris was awarded a National Aboriginal Achievement Award for his research on water treatment in a northern Manitoban Aboriginal community.

IN, AND OUT AGAIN

Cynthia Mackenzie

■ ■ ■

Eenie meenie miney mo
Catch a tiger by the toe
If he hollers let him go
Eenie meenie miney mo

WHEN I WAS seven I came home from school one day telling a different version of this traditional nursery
rhyme. Instead of catching a tiger by the toe, I sang
about catching a nigger by the toe. I had lived in Canada my
whole life, in a typical northern town: small—with a population of only 1,500—and isolated. I had no idea what "nigger"
meant. In fact, I didn't even know what people looked like if
they weren't white.

My parents sat me down that day and told me the meaning
of that word. That discussion deeply affected me. It wasn't just
that the word "nigger" was derogatory or that it had a history

of oppression. To Mom and Dad, the word was awful because it was isolating—it kept some people "in" and some people "out." All I could figure out then was that if you were a nigger, you were definitely out.

That nursery rhyme was one of my first experiences with the power of exclusion in an otherwise peaceful small-town childhood: I grew up spending hours with my friends exploring forests of beautiful lodgepole pine trees and vast expanses of wilderness. But as I grew older I moved several times with my family, and I encountered many more incidences of exclusion. In junior high I had a friend from the only Asian family in town; instead of calling her by her name, everyone just called her "the Oriental girl." I stopped talking to an Aboriginal friend because my classmates told me not to speak to people like her. I had high-school friends who listened to *Brocket 99*, a spoof radio show in which voices purported to be from an Aboriginal community and played up stereotypes of Native peoples. My friends loved it, but I cringed every time I heard it.

These isolating, racist incidents are the darker side of my youth, and they are some of my most vivid memories. I learned that stereotypes and names ensured that there was an *us* and a really clear *them*. "They" always seemed to have labels so that we could pick them out easily: nigger, Indian, Oriental. These words came to me casually as a kid, but even then I understood that they had a profound power to exclude. They clearly implied that some people just didn't belong in our community. These words distilled a world of beautiful, vibrant difference into a single, simple, negative "them."

As I grew up and moved from one Prairie community to another, I learned that to fit in, I needed to figure out what others considered normal and how I could be the same as everyone else. I joined clubs, did well at school, made friends, and actively minimized my differences and hid my opinions. I didn't question the need to be the same—I just knew that if I didn't quickly learn what the kids around me were listening to, what they were saying, and who their friends were, I, too, would be isolated and excluded.

It was a useful strategy through grade school. I spent my childhood morphing into what was acceptable and didn't stand up for my own differences or for those friends who were excluded. I didn't question my classmates about listening to *Brocket 99*—I just stopped hanging around with them. I didn't keep my friendship with a fourteen-year-old Aboriginal girl when I was challenged—I just shut up.

Now that I'm an adult I feel I have a responsibility to do better. I have a responsibility to respect differences so that other people, especially those who look different and speak different, don't feel the same kind of pressure to compromise their distinctiveness or to "blend in" with me and the communities I belong to that I felt when I was younger. I have a responsibility to give voice to the little girl I was, who adapted, became intimidated by uniqueness, and downplayed her differences. And I have a responsibility to give voice to the excluded friends of my childhood.

Perhaps because of this sense of responsibility, I began volunteering at a clinic in my hometown, and I started travelling, which sparked my interest in working in community development. I first left home and the comforts of all that I knew when I was seventeen. En route to Costa Rica, I travelled through Toronto. It was my first time in a big city, and there I saw two things for the first time in my life: a subway system and a homeless man. I suppose both are rather unremarkable for urban dwellers, but growing up in a rural community, I'd never before taken public transportation and had never witnessed absolute poverty.

If my childhood communities excluded others, the city seemed to carry out exclusion on an exceptionally, incomprehensibly grand scale. My community judged those who were different, but I'd never before seen a person sleeping on a sidewalk, and I had never seen a panhandler. The man on the street in Toronto asked me for money, and I wanted to talk to him, but I couldn't. I was scared of him. I was so shocked at seeing a homeless man that I didn't know what to say; my fellow travellers were mostly from cities, and I felt hopelessly naive.

I believe it was in witnessing the scale of this exclusion, combined with my volunteer work, that compelled me to act on a bigger scale. I started to see how I could use my life to be of service, to work with others, to be involved in cross-cultural community development projects, and to teach youth from diverse backgrounds and cultures. I also started to recognize my true self: I began to accept my own different, inconvenient opinions and my own unpopular ideas.

In Costa Rica that year I volunteered for four months in a community called Santa Elena, where I worked with twelve international volunteers in the rain forest developing an eco-tourist reserve and wildlife research station. I fell in love with the country and the region. I've since worked in Guatemala and Cuba, and I've travelled through parts of Honduras, Belize, Mexico, and Nicaragua. I returned to Costa Rica years later and served for a year there as a team leader on various community projects: I catalogued a new species of bat in the southern peninsula and assisted conservationists dedicated to leatherback sea turtle release. I also did back-breaking labour digging miles of aqueduct trenches, constructing a biological conservation post on the Nicaraguan border, and digging the foundation for a health post in an isolated Aboriginal mountain community. Each of these projects involved groups of twelve young people from around the world—including Canada—speaking Spanish, learning the Quechua language of the *indios*, and experiencing the delight of eating rice and starchy bananas for breakfast.

I am still young, and I continue to volunteer and travel at every opportunity I can find—to Latin America, India, Europe, Australia, and the Caribbean. With each experience, I have felt a renewed passion for the beauty of difference and a renewed passion to give something back to the place I live in. My drive has become less about being angry at the imperfections that exist in communities and more about engaging with others to build the community around us into something better: I have volunteered in my community's social support organizations, become involved with countless social justice initiatives on my university campus, organized human rights campaigns, and worked with international students. And maybe most important, I have learned how to talk about what I hope for: a community that finds solidarity and support in its similarities and that honours and respects its members' diversity and uniqueness.

In 1998 I was invited to give a talk at a conference on the United Nations' 50th Anniversary of the Declaration of Human Rights. There, I spoke about youth engagement and about how community service is something that our generation not only is capable of doing, but also needs to do more of. It's our liminal space—our opportunity to assume our adult responsibilities in the world.

Archbishop Desmond Tutu was the keynote speaker at the conference, and he spoke about community as an orchestra. He said that everyone fits into the music making and is crucial to the playing of the symphony—even the tiny "ting" of the triangle player. (He said this, beautifully, while all five feet of him ran across the stage as the conductor in his analogy— quite an accomplishment for an elderly man!) Desmond Tutu used his voice and his story to bring acceptance of difference to South Africa in the time of apartheid, when the insidiousness of sameness and the polarization of difference could not have been more stark.

In my volunteer work I have continually seen the profundity of Archbishop Tutu's analogy: community isn't a uniform "us" for other people to either fit into or to be excluded from. The orchestra doesn't work when it's composed only of violins or when we refuse to include the audience, the stage crew, the sound manager, the production team, and the instrument tuners. It's in the totality of very different roles that the enterprise functions. When difference exists, we have a choice: to accept it into our community, refuse it, or attempt to convert it so that it becomes the same as "us." But understanding can't be based on either exclusion or co-option. Community has to be based on difference itself.

I've learned to tell my own story—this story—as a way of sharing my doubts and challenges, my hopes and dreams. Storytelling is the perfect medium for community building. A community will only work if each voice counts, and to count, all voices must be heard. I've come to believe that it's a powerfully violent act to silence the voices of others, and that to have an inclusive community, all of its members must listen to one another.

I think that community is a conscious and continuous act, not an end goal to be achieved. And so I try to approach my community now as a process or an opportunity: It's a daily decision to fight our tendency to slot people as "out." It's a daily decision to be aware of exclusion and to challenge it through the power of storytelling and listening. It's a daily decision I make to promote inclusion and to draw strength from our diversity.

CYNTHIA MACKENZIE has helped organize and manage numerous human rights initiatives, including advocating for refugees, developing ethics-based curricula for social justice work, and facilitating local community-building initiatives. She has been recognized by Volunteer Calgary as a Leader of Tomorrow and by *Maclean's* magazine as one of Canada's 100 Faces of the Future. She has a background in international community development and has managed the Pacifica Centre at the Lester B. Pearson College in Victoria, British Columbia. She is currently studying towards her doctorate in politics in Melbourne, Australia.

Devi Mucina

I WAS BORN IN 1972, though I don't know the exact date of my birth. My baba (father) believes it was in October.

Baba trekked from Malawi, where he was born, down to South Africa. It was a long, extremely difficult journey. When Baba arrived, he encountered so much racism he trekked back up north to Zimbabwe. There, he was introduced to my amai (mother), whose family lived on the Chendambya reserves, forced there by the white colonial settlers who stole their lands.

My parents' is not the typical Western love story, but it is the Bantu way. Traditionally, marriage is a functional, very practical arrangement. My amai was from a caring family that was very connected to its culture and identity, which was what Baba was looking for. So a friend approached her elders, spoke on my baba's behalf around 1970, and in 1971 they were married.

They had three kids, in what order I'm not aware, though I know I'm the only one who survived. In 1974 my parents separated. The circumstances have never been clear to me, but I do know that they parted ways during Zimbabwe's war of national liberation. Life would have been difficult for Baba and his countrymen then: they were labelled as traitors in the fight against black oppression because they served as cheap labour for the colonial government of Rhodesia, which the majority of Zimbabweans would not work for. On top of this issue Baba worked in the city of Harare and could only see the family when he had time off work—about once a month if he was lucky. Because Baba was from Malawi, he didn't have a homestead to offer Amai, so she stayed with her family. Thus, they were strangers who were married, and their colonial reality left them with little room to build a relationship.

After the separation Amai's parents told Baba, "You need to come and get your child." I can't imagine the kind of stress this unexpected burden generated for Baba. His marriage was over, and he had custody of a two-year-old child. He owned no home, had no family in the country, and was dependent on part-time domestic labour jobs, an employment arrangement I now call neo-slavery. He was suddenly faced with the challenge of first finding us a place to sleep and next making sure that we avoided overstaying our welcome. My earliest memories revolve around this change in our lives.

I clearly remember sitting on a gravel street. There is a pink building behind me, probably the grocery store. And there are women on the street selling produce. I'm sitting, asleep, and when I wake up, I notice that I have peed on Baba's suit. And he's just irate, he's fuming, he's holding me at arm's length, and he's yelling out of frustration. A woman comes and offers to help. And my father says, "Well, I think I need to get used to this. It's just he and I."

For the first four years I moved from family to family, and I never really lived with my father. We were really poor, and he would get work as a domestic worker, a "house boy" cook or gardener for different white households. But he was never allowed to keep a child on their premises. Every now and then I would live with him hidden in the servants' quarters.

Eventually Baba found a job as a gardener with a small family in Mabelreign, at the time a white suburb of Harare. At first he kept me hidden. But eventually his employers discovered me. When they heard Baba's story, they let me run around the community freely as their ward. That's when I learned to speak English. I spent all my time with the other white kids in the neighbourhood. At first I believed we were friends, but as I got older I learned I was their black play toy. White kids went to school, and I didn't because their schools were white-only, and without a birth certificate, I couldn't even go to the African township schools.

Wanting and wishing to be privileged like the whites, I convinced Baba to take a new job as a cook with one of my toy masters' parents. They seemed wonderful, and I thought it would be a better job for Baba. But it was a terrible mistake. One day I was helping the "baas" (boss) when his wife brought us some juice. I must have made gulping noises as I drank, because he yelled, "You sip it—you don't gulp it down. That sounds like a monkey! Don't Africans know how to drink?" I was so angry, so humiliated, yet I felt so powerless. I was nothing.

As I told Baba about my experience his face betrayed shame, which became sadness, which became anger—and finally his face was awash with nothing but pain. It was the way he slowly shook his head and heavily sighed that told to me I was travelling a well-worn path of racism in Southern Africa.

For some time after we left that family we stayed in an abandoned building. Our relationship became strained. I was always running around and getting into trouble, and he had difficulty getting neo-slavery work and was on edge. He became quite abusive whenever he disciplined me. My response was always to run away. He'd become more stern, and I'd run away more. I'd stay in the bushes and woods. As a runaway I eventually moved in my search for food to a community where there were more businesses, which is how I ended up in the suburb of Marlborough. I slept in a wastepaper bin, scavenged for food, and ate from the garbage bins of stores and restaurants. I would try to get money from white women by offering to carry their grocery bags—white men were only nice when they were with their mothers, girlfriends, or wives.

I guess one of the African workers there noticed that I was sleeping in the wastepaper bin. He informed his employer, an older Greek woman, and she summoned me. She asked if I'd eaten anything recently. I said no, and she fed me. She got me a T-shirt; I remember it read, "Vote for Mugabe." I wouldn't tell her who I was or where I came from, so she called in social services. After some searching social services found Baba, but after about three months of not seeing me, the first words from Baba's mouth were, "If you leave him here I will kill him." So I became a ward of the state.

Baba and I grew further and further apart, but fortunately we never lost touch. For a long time I was angry and resentful, but I knew he was the only family I had. I retained a spiritual connection with him: I would dream about him when he was sick. We'd have intimate moments discussing and interpreting our dreams. In some ways we were close, and in other ways we were miles apart—there was always an ambivalent intimate connection. I never met Amai, although with the support of Baba I asked people around me to write to her on my behalf. Members of her family came to see me, but my amai never did.

Meanwhile, since I spoke English almost like a first language the state put me in a mostly white orphanage. I had three square meals, a bed, my own sheets, a towel—I felt I'd gotten into heaven. I was safe and excited to go to school. And I felt privileged to be admitted into this white society.

It was when the orphanage, St. Joseph's House for Boys, sent me to school that I realized there was trouble—I couldn't read or write. My education until then had always been interrupted, and I'd never been to school full-time. I had all kinds of psychological evaluations. I became a series of walking labels, and "brain-damaged" became the most prominent of these labels. As the labels grew in number, the staff intervened less and less until, finally, nobody was helping me. So I put my energy into sports—first boxing and then rugby.

As time passed my problems with school brought me down. I wasn't learning to read or write. And deep within me I felt growing guilt, resentment, and anger at my failure to perform a basic skill that everyone else in the orphanage could grasp. I thought, "Why me?" I was taking up a spot that another African could have used to do something great, to help the community. That feeling got stronger as I got older: why am *I* being given this break if I can't use it to its full potential? I thought of so many African kids who would have really loved an opportunity to learn, and as much as I wanted to, I couldn't capitalize on mine. I had tried everything in my power to learn to read and write: I had taken every test they gave me, I had gone to the special classes, I'd stayed up studying until the early hours of the morning, but still I couldn't crack the secret to reading and writing.

When I understood the concepts underlying what we were studying—as I did in math and science, for example—I was great. My love for learning was evident to most teachers, but still, I always failed every test I took. Some teachers thought I was really bright, so they took my blank exam papers as evidence that I was not being challenged enough. Others thought I was lazy but had potential. Yet nobody ever clued in to the fact that I couldn't read or write. As much as I wanted to participate in my education, I couldn't.

I started to feel alone. In the orphanage I grew aware that the white kids were the ones being adopted, no matter how many problems they had, whereas a black child was never adopted. We blacks realized that our life in the orphanage was the best it would ever be for us. Even then we tried to conform to the standards of the white community and be a part of it.

I suffered a lot of oppression in the orphanage when I participated in activities that were supposed to offer me better opportunities. I went away on holiday camps organized by white Christian missionaries. They called converting us to Christians "giving us spiritual salvation," but I now know it was an effort to kill our spirituality. However, the extracurricular excursions weren't all bad. Some programs did nurture my leadership qualities and skills, like Journey of a Lifetime, which took me and other disadvantaged or disabled children on an extraordinary month-long expedition as a way of empowering us. I also participated in the Outward Bound (OB) program, an experiential wilderness course in which youth learn about leadership, teamwork, and respect for the environment.

Meanwhile, I continued to be involved in sports. Rugby was very good to me. I was always the youngest player on my teams, and people had hopes I'd eventually play at the national level. It was through rugby that I first went to Europe. After our school team, Prince Edward, finished its UK tour I was able to move in with an English couple I'd met in Africa through Journey of a Lifetime. I stayed with them in England for a year; they were a great family. But I still had a sense I was at their mercy. What happened if I screwed up? I knew I had to be a contributing member of society, but I'd only seen what Baba did and could only conceive of doing menial work. The family would ask me what I wanted to do, and I had no idea. I realized I needed to find myself. To everybody's horror, I decided to go home to St. Joseph's.

When I got back to the orphanage, my changing thoughts about my identity and the colonial system reached a new level.

When I was in England I realized that Europe wasn't a dreamy, perfect place. I started to see that white people had it great in Africa: they could be masters there and have privileges and powers they could never have anywhere else. I also began to acknowledge that even in Europe people suffered. So the ideas of white superiority that the colonialists were selling us didn't turn out to be facts at all.

When I talked about my African spirituality at St. Joseph's, the other kids laughed and teased me for being "African." When I was fifteen, I started to ask myself what our African traditions had to offer. And when I got back from Europe and started taking these ideas much more seriously, I began to educate the young kids in the orphanage by telling them, "What they're telling you isn't right. Your name, your culture—these things make you special and give you your grounding, which you can't get anywhere else."

Formal schooling had not worked for me, so I decided to try my luck at working in experiential education; I applied for a job with Outward Bound, remembering that I had done well in my OB course in Chimanimani. To complete my job application, I went around St. Joseph's asking each of my brothers—other boys—to help me spell one or two words. This way I was able to save face and still get the application and résumé done.

My educational level was well below what OB required, so the warden, Fen Goodes, offered me an apprenticeship with

one condition: I had to keep working on improving my education, especially since I was expected to read and write reports.
To help me, Fen said, "Here's what we're going to do. I'm going
to give you each word that you can't spell, and we'll put them
all in this big chart."

I studied this list, but I could never phonetically break up
and retain the words. So I pasted the words all over my apartment. I covered my kitchen with positive words; another room
would have words for negative characteristics; and in the hall-
way I had connecting words. I used this strategy to write my
reports.

While I was at OB I ran courses for elementary and high
schools; I helped create and implement the first OB course in
Africa for disabled students; and I taught management and
team-building courses for companies in Zimbabwe. I also
managed to play club rugby and coach at a school. In my final
year at OB Zimbabwe I met Karen, a Canadian woman who was
also an instructor with OB. We started dating, and she sponsored me to come to Canada and helped me make connections with the western Canadian branch of OB. Before I left for
North America I did a stint in South Africa, where I had a great
experience running one of the first programs to bring together
youth from different political backgrounds. It was empowering
to be a part of making positive change in South Africa. Unfortunately I could only stay there for six months, since my plans
for immigrating to Canada were already set. I came to Canada
in 1994 and in the same year married Karen.

My marriage ended pretty quickly, and I moved on from
Outward Bound. Through rugby connections I became involved
in community development, and soon I was working as a youth
and family counsellor for the Vancouver School Board. As I
gained more confidence in myself, I became more adventurous,
so around 1998, I decided to give literacy another shot.

I think I called the number off of one of those ads for adult literacy. I was referred to a program where the teacher, Janet Kuper, suggested I write about my own experiences—she was fascinated by the stories I told her about my life. I can remember her saying, "I only want to hear about your stories through your writing, and I expect you to write something every day." I've always loved a good challenge, and any success, no matter how small, seems to give me more confidence every time. Using the skills I learned working with Janet, I set a goal to get my high-school diploma by the end of the year. Janet was skeptical, but with a little luck and a lot of hard work I passed.

Shortly afterwards I started a counselling certificate program at Vancouver Community College; to gain access to more support for my education, I was required to undergo another psychological evaluation. I learned that I was dyslexic and became entitled to disability support. After I earned my counselling certificate, I completed a program to get a social service worker certificate. Then I did a B.A. in human and social development studying child and youth care at the University of Victoria. As soon as I completed my bachelor's degree I started my master's in dispute resolution but soon realized that the program wasn't the best fit for me, so I transferred into the M.A. program for indigenous governance, which I completed in 2006, also at the University of Victoria.

During the time I've spent in Canada I've learned so much about the concept of home, and this new appreciation has allowed me to love where I come from, to understand my culture, and to get to know my people and myself.

I have become aware that, in Africa, there are alternatives to what the colonial system has taught us. When the white colonial system imposed and prescribed a lifestyle on us, we started losing our culture, our identity, our religions, our ways of knowing, our environment, and our education. I know now that the colonial system can only lead to the betterment of the colonial people, because they made it to serve themselves. It can never help us; it can only create division among us.

Today I still see Africans that reflect the kind of child that I was—hopeless, confused, disoriented. White society told me what to believe, and I saw white people as masters. I was afraid of white people and didn't dare defy them. And that mindset is what they have convinced us is right; we need to challenge this kind of education. I know it's a lot of work to build ourselves up again from within. But then I think to myself, if I'm not going to do it, who will? If I'm not willing to risk my own live-lihood and financial security to build an African destiny that we determine ourselves and that is not determined by West-erners, how can I ask someone else to do it? I know that the moment I take on this challenge, I will see people like me take up the fight for our freedom.

An example of the action that I am taking to reclaim our heritage and determine our future using our values and knowl-edge can be found in my master's thesis, *Revitalizing Memory in Honour of Maseko Ngoni's Indigenous Bantu Governance*, in which I use geopolitical, linguistic, and oral histories to demonstrate how the personal memories of the Maseko Ngoni people can be used to create a resurgence and regeneration of indigenous Bantu governance.

When I complete my education I want to go home and work in Zimbabwe, Malawi, South Africa, and other parts of Africa—but not just there. I want to travel to places like India to see how other communities have dealt with colonialism. Can we, the so-called natives of imperial colonialism, support each other?

There's one more truth I've realized. We have to be gen-tle with ourselves. Colonialism is all about oppressing us and making us feel inferior. Thus, we need to start empowering our own families and ourselves by using traditional knowledge. We also need to talk about some of the shameful things that colonialism has made us do because it is only through confronting this shame, while embracing what is authentically ours, that we'll be able to forgive our own relatives and our own peoples for their parts in the abuses perpetrated through colonialism.

I look at my own experience and see how angry I was at Baba and Amai because they had failed to protect me. But now, when I consider the colonial context of oppression and enslavement, I understand their responses in relation to the constant colonial effort to make them inferior. My understanding of these dynamics helps me fight the tendencies of self-hatred that colonialism creates.

With hope, pride, and respect for our brothers and sisters and all that is Bantu, we can move forward.

■ ■ ■ ■ ■

DEVI MUCINA has been an instructor for Outward Bound (www. outwardbound.net) in Zimbabwe, South Africa, and Canada; an alternative program and youth and family worker with the Vancouver School Board; camp director and manager of the Haven Society for abused women and children; and a counsellor with the Maples Adolescent Treatment Centre. Currently he coordinates a violence intervention program offered by East Metro Youth Services at Cedarbrae Collegiate Institute. He holds a certificate in counselling skills, a social service worker certificate, a B.A. in human and social development (child and youth care), and an M.A. in indigenous governance. He hopes to acquire a Ph.D. in education.

WRITING THE WRONG

Ben Peterson

■
 ■
■

I HAVE SOMETHING TO confess to you up front: I'm a male
WASP. Born into a loving upper-middle-class family, I had
few worries. None of my parents' friends, family, or neighbours ever had to use a food bank or struggle to find shelter for
the night, and my classmates were pretty much in the same
boat. There were a handful of rough kids at school, but their
world was so foreign to me that I never really bonded with
them—and unfortunately, most of them dropped out of school
or were expelled by the end of grade ten.

Like a good little WASP, I got my B.A. and a master's degree
to boot. Throughout my studies, I went through the motions of
"involvement" like most keeners. I attended model parliaments
and model UNs, and I sat on student government committees.
Although I didn't realize it at the time, I pretended to be more
involved than I really was. It was more a means to a selfish

end—to meet people, be respected, and pad my résumé—than of effecting real change. I was still oblivious to the difficulties those outside my bubble faced. Not getting into a bar was a tragedy—war and famine in Africa were an afterthought.

After I finished school I applied for a job in Ghana, West Africa, to write government reports to the UN on various international human rights treaties. I applied on a whim, thinking I had little chance of being hired. Although I'd taken a course on human rights during my master's program and spent a summer working for Lloyd Axworthy, then the Canadian minister of foreign affairs, I felt I had no business even considering the job. I didn't know much about Africa or what an international human rights treaty really was. But I thought, "Why not get paid to travel?"

MY SIX MONTHS in Ghana rocked me to my core.

I didn't know exactly what I would encounter when I arrived, but after seeing a thousand pictures of emaciated African families and World Vision commercials asking us to "adopt" starving children from afar, I guess I was partly expecting to meet sufferers void of humanity. Instead, I found people exactly like you and me, with remarkable intelligence and an indomitable human spirit. The Ghanaians shared a proud and profound history, and they valued family bonds and relationships above material goods, in stark contrast to Canadian consumerist culture. They brimmed with patience, respect, humility, and contentment with what they had—not anger at what they didn't have. In Ghana I made lifelong friends and quickly realized that I had more to learn from their society than I could ever bring to them.

But juxtaposed with this idealistic, almost naive understanding of Ghanaian culture was the suffering of many of its people. Throughout my stay I worked for Ghana's Ministry of Justice, writing reports to the UN on the Convention on the Elimination of All Forms of Racial Discrimination and on the Convention on the Rights of the Child. I investigated Ghana's compliance with UN standards its government had previously agreed to meet. This work exposed me to a depressing array of human rights abuses that occurred daily. I saw incidents of child slavery, human trafficking, ethnic violence, religious discrimination, child labour, gross domestic violence, and countless other atrocities.

I met Adwoa, a young Ghanaian woman staying at a hospital in Accra. She had been violently raped and became infected with HIV as a result. Being sexually assaulted made Adwoa a pariah, and her family abandoned her. She had been fighting her disease for about a year at the hospital, which served as nothing more than a place for her to die. Helpless doctors looked on as their patients, including Adwoa, suffered without medicine or food. Occasionally a family member would bring her a meal of kenkey, a dish made from fermented corn, or she would get a shot of penicillin when it was in stock. Her body was defenceless against the onslaught of AIDS.

I walked into her hospital room and saw a thin bed wrapped in plastic sheets surrounded by bare, exposed concrete walls. Adwoa, skinny to the bone, was sitting on her bed wearing nothing but a soiled cloth around her loins. She had been passing in and out of delirium but was lucid when I arrived. "Welcome," she said, pointing to her kenkey. I didn't reply—I couldn't. She offered me her only food, while I had enough money in my pocket for at least a few days of medication that could have, if only temporarily, saved her from her pain.

Misconceptions about HIV and AIDS lead society to react in ways that can prove harmful to the disease's sufferers. I couldn't help but think that if Adwoa had lived in a community that respected her rights as someone battling AIDS, her story would have been dramatically different. She wouldn't have been stigmatized to the same extent, and her family wouldn't have disowned her, leaving her to the gut-wrenching local health system. They and local health officials would have given her more of the support she needed to combat the disease, and she could have been put through life-improving antiretroviral therapy.

After meeting countless others like Adwoa, I came to believe that the best way to protect the rights of these average citizens is to increase public awareness and acceptance of human rights, something that could be effectively achieved via the local media. For example, drawing attention to Adwoa's plight could have prompted the Ghanaian government and civil society groups to ensure adequate care for Adwoa and others suffering with HIV/AIDS. When local African media report effectively on human rights issues, they inform people about their own rights in a cultural context that they understand. They also pressure the government to improve its human rights record. And when progress occurs simultaneously on the governmental and grassroots levels, ideal conditions for substantial change are created.

With this thought in mind, I co-founded Journalists for Human Rights (JHR) with Alexandra Sicotte Leveque, a friend and colleague living in Côte d'Ivoire at the time, to help local African media report more effectively on human rights issues. JHR currently works in nine African countries—Ghana, Benin, Senegal, Uganda, Nigeria, Sierra Leone, Tanzania, South African, and Namibia—to provide human rights information to 20 million people each week through local media sources.

In each country JHR runs a variety of projects to provide local journalists and editors with the skills and incentives to report on human rights. In our most important and innovative program we begin by forming partnerships with the most influential newspapers, radio stations, and TV stations in a given country. We then send journalism trainers into their newsrooms to work alongside local journalists for up to eight months at a time. Our trainers don't do any reporting themselves, but they train local journalists through every step of the journalism process. In return for this training, JHR asks its partners to set aside a certain amount of print space or air time for human rights stories, thus ensuring that human rights issues get attention.

JHR also implements programs to foster sustainable change. We forge networks of journalists interested in human rights, we train journalism professors, we establish human rights reporting awards in partnership with local media associations, and we coach African journalists to conduct training on our behalf. Every activity is designed to have a lasting impact, creating change long after JHR leaves. In fact, JHR works in each country for at most five years—we aim to encourage change without making local journalists dependent on our work.

Our approach is in contrast to traditional NGO approaches to international human rights issues. Many of the big players in this realm, like the United Nations, develop human rights policies. Others, like Amnesty International, pressure governments to improve domestic human rights situations. But by working with local African media JHR is able to rally mass support for human rights within the countries where the worst abuses are taking place. By producing stories on people like Adwoa, JHR empowers average citizens to take control of their lives.

JHR has also started twenty-two chapters at universities across Canada. These chapters bring like-minded students together, where they collaborate to run media-driven human rights awareness campaigns. For example, JHR-Ryerson successfully pressured their school administration to change their paper supplier after exposing the fact that their old supplier's logging operations violated First Nations land rights, and JHR-Alberta ran human rights workshops at local high schools. With 20 per cent of Canadian journalism students now members of JHR's chapters, the organization will be a positive force in influencing how our media view domestic and international human rights in the years to come.

The years since JHR's birth haven't been easy. It has been difficult to get funding, to be considered credible at my young age (I was twenty-four when I started JHR), to get charitable status, to figure out how to actually start an organization and how the hell to run it. Call it trial by fire.

What's allowed me to get through the barrage of difficulties and doubts is a combination of two things. First, I believe passionately in the work that JHR does. Our programs have been successful, visibly changing the way the media, particularly in Ghana, report on human rights. JHR has trained over 35 per cent of all journalists in Ghana and has produced stories that have exposed rapists and helped child labourers. JHR's work also prompted the first ever official public forum on gay rights held in Ghana, a country in which homosexuality is still illegal. The Ghana Journalists Association, which represents over 90 per cent of journalists in the country, has endorsed our work, saying "JHR is offering an invaluable service not only to journalists, but also to the general public who benefit tremendously."

My second source of motivation comes from my belief that we're obligated to come to the assistance of those less fortunate than us, no matter where in the world they live. If Adwoa had been born in Canada she'd be living a far more comfortable and fulfilling life, even with HIV and AIDS. Instead, she suffered in a way most of us can't contemplate. We have the money, skills, and resources to prevent this kind of misery. Is it moral to ignore the plight of people like Adwoa when we can put a stop to their suffering?

■ ■ ■ ■ ■

BEN PETERSON is the co-founder and executive director of Journalists for Human Rights (www.jhr.ca). Ben has also worked for Ghana's Ministry of Justice; for the former Canadian minister of foreign affairs, Lloyd Axworthy; and in the offices of David Bonior, the former Democratic whip in the United States House of Representatives. Ben is an Action Canada fellow (2004–05). He has a B.A. in Economics and a B.A.H. in Political Studies from Queen's University, and an M.Sc. in Political Theory from the London School of Economics.

FINDING THE "I"
IN ACTION:
DEFINING ACTIVISM
TO INCLUDE ME

Natalie Gerum

WHEN I SAY the word "activist," what do you think of? A red bandana, a smoke bomb, and a placard for change? A blockade across a logging road, with people chained to trees as bulldozers inch closer? Or do you think of a straight-A student with a role in the school play, a seat in the jazz band, and a position on the student council? I didn't, either. The bandana and the smoke bomb—that's how I defined activism. And it wasn't how I defined myself.

Growing up in Hamilton, Ontario, I was a good student, and good students weren't activists—good students couldn't be activists. We didn't speak out against authority or go to protests or challenge policy; we followed the rules, respected our teachers, and accepted the status quo. I didn't want to participate in organizations that were considered fringe and fanatical, because I knew the adults in my life would disapprove. And the actions these groups took scared me: they seemed so pushy, so aggressive. Tear gas and riot squads—those had nothing to do with me.

Environmentalism, especially, *really* had nothing to do with me. Environmental activists were always the ones on the evening news facing off against police squads. Not only did they prompt a few disapproving headlines each week, but they also talked about issues I'd never learned about in school or at home. Of all the activist issues, I identified least with environmental concerns. Environmentalists had the bandanas plus beards and bare feet. No, I was a good student, and all I wanted was to one day become a good teacher.

Then, I kicked off my shoes. In the summer of 2002 I participated in the Pearson Seminar on Youth Leadership (PSYL) in Victoria, British Columbia. Every year PSYL brings together 120 youth from across Canada and around the globe and encourages them to explore and develop skills that will help them become future community and world leaders. At PSYL I expected to meet presidents of student councils, food bank volunteers, and people who taught swimming lessons—people like me. I most definitely didn't expect to meet an activist on my first night there. We were all sitting on the lawn of one of the dormitories, getting to know each other and telling stories. All of a sudden, this girl started talking about protests she'd been to and what it was like to be tear-gassed and dragged away by riot squads. She used acronyms I didn't understand and talked about trade agreements and international policies I'd never heard of. She was incredibly informed, well-spoken, and knowledgeable— and I was totally intimidated. This girl fell right into my definition of activism; everything she talked about was what I avoided. Yet she was articulate, thoughtful, and friendly. I went to bed that night very anxious about the next three weeks. Did everybody else there have stories like that girl's?

I went to the opening presentation of the seminar scared that I'd stick out, that someone would realize I didn't really understand why the United States was invading Iraq, or didn't know what areas of British Columbia were being clear-cut, or couldn't list the companies that used child labour. It was one of the only times in my life I've sat in the back row, and the only time during PSYL, because after the first day, everything in my universe changed, including me.

Over the next three weeks we participated in interactive workshops, simulation exercises, and creative activities run by the program coordinators and took in a series of presentations by guest speakers from a variety of movements for change. Lyndsay was one of our first presenters. "The media doesn't get it," she said when she started her workshop. She had pink hair, and she'd started her own organization about critical thinking, media, and globalization when she was nineteen. She was so articulate, so informed—and she was an activist. I could relate to what she was saying, though—it made sense to me. Before I heard her speak, globalization was a word I had heard once in a while, but I never understood what it meant or how it was relevant to me. Globalization, Lyndsay explained, affected who controlled the media and what information was made available to citizens. And the media influenced how I perceived the world. I learned that globalization, an "activist issue," mattered in my life.

I began to see that I was connected to activist issues, but I still didn't know much about them, and I was apprehensive about my ignorance. Where was I supposed to begin to learn what's wrong with the world and how to fix it? Not having the knowledge about global issues was another barrier to my becoming involved in effecting change.

But at PSYL I learned not to be ashamed of how little I knew. In her workshop about water privatization in Bolivia, Sheelagh, our coordinator, asked us, "What happens to the provision of a service once it's privatized?" That question would once have sent me running for the safety of the back row, but I felt I was in a safe space at the seminar, free to ask as many questions as I wanted and to begin becoming informed. It wasn't too late to start learning about water privatization and other global issues. It wasn't too late to become active—but I still wasn't prepared to become an activist.

Even though I began to see how activist issues related to me and knew that I could get informed about these issues, I couldn't get over the negative connotations of the word "activist" or those images of belligerent protesters on the evening news. However, I soon learned that those smoke bombs and bulldozers had nothing to do with one of Canada's most well-respected activists.

Dr. Mary Wynne-Ashford is a member of Physicians for Global Survival, an anti-nuclear organization working to abolish nuclear weapons. On the anniversary of the nuclear bombing of Nagasaki in World War II, she came to PSYL to give a presentation on her involvement in the movement to abolish nuclear armaments. This incredibly educated woman didn't fit my stereotype of an activist—she was a grandmother and a doctor. But she actively demonstrated and spoke out against nuclear weapons and dedicated her life to creating a safer world. Her activism wasn't intimidating; it was empowering, and it made me realize that there were many kinds of activism—and activists. What I had seen on the news was only one, very biased, portrayal of activists; the smoke bombs the media showed were really a smoke screen of prevailing anti-activist sentiment. I realized that it takes all different kinds of people to make change, and I could be one of those people. I could be an activist.

After PSYL I could no longer accept that it was wrong to stand up and take action for what I believed in. At the seminar I'd built incredible relationships with all kinds of activists. These individuals weren't wrong—they were doing the right thing to build a better world.

Throughout PSYL we'd taken on Mahatma Gandhi's challenge to humanity: to be the change that we wanted to see in the world. At the end of those three weeks I realized those words were a call to activism, a world that included Lyndsay and Sheelagh and Dr. Ashford—and could even include me. I learned not only that global issues affect me, but also, and more important, that *I* could affect these issues if I chose to.

I also became much better informed. Before the seminar, I wouldn't have known where to find information about contemporary global issues; PSYL afforded me an "in." After that summer I felt that by learning about these activist issues, I'd taken a first step towards making change and taking action, and the next steps came much more easily.

I have come to think of activism as twofold: it means *being* the change, actively leading a life that reflects the kind of world you want to live in, and it's about creating action beyond yourself and acting as an agent of change. It's about believing in something so passionately that you can't just contain it within your own life; you want, need, feel a responsibility to share it with others—your family, your friends, your community, your government, your world. Activism is action that happens on both a personal and a public level, and I was ready to make activism part of my life.

As I redefined activism to include myself, I also needed to redefine my life to include activism. I still wanted to be a teacher, but now I wanted to facilitate for others the kind of experience I had at PSYL, where I felt I'd received a much more relevant education than I had ever gotten at my school. I realized that for education to truly create positive change, it needed to nurture agents of change. It needed to give students an "in" to learning about global issues and affirm that activism wasn't wrong. As I searched for a chance to further develop these ideas about education, I remembered that two of our coordinators from PSYL, Meredith and Mark, worked for an outdoor school in B.C., and I knew that anything these two incredible individuals were involved with had to be worth checking out.

Based out of British Columbia's Sunshine Coast, Sea to Sky Outdoor School for Sustainability Education is a leader in environmental and experiential education in Canada. Recognizing the need to empower students to become conscientious actors, not only on environmental issues, but also in life, Sea to Sky welcomes school groups from across southern British Columbia each year during the spring and fall to embrace the ideals of community, leadership, and action in the hope of shifting our society towards a more sustainable future.

After just four days of volunteering on one of the school's island sites, I was overwhelmed by inspiration: students were engaged in what they were learning; the teachers, known as "Islanders," were a co-operative, creative, and committed team of educators; and the school community dynamically fused a love for learning and a love for the earth. My plans for the future shifted significantly following my time at Sea to Sky.

Environmentalism had been the final frontier of activism for me—even after PSYL I still found it daunting. I realize now that my discomfort with it had nothing to do with beards and bare feet and everything to do with my having no desire to incorporate environmentalism into my life. I was comfortable with my daily habits and didn't want to make sacrifices. But

194

at Sea to Sky, we were all living in a way that was completely compatible with environmental consciousness: I was composting, stagger-showering, and eating vegetarian. And it was empowering. Just as PSYL had been my "in" to activism, Sea to Sky was my "in" to environmentalism. I came to recognize my connection to the earth, I saw how my choices affected the planet, and I realized that although I was part of the problem, I could be part of the solution—my engagement made a difference. The Sea to Sky approach towards sustainability wasn't mainstream, but I wasn't alone in adopting it, either. I now understood, after having lived and learned beside the amazing Islander team, that I had support in my ambitions from a whole community of folks choosing to live more lightly on the earth.

I knew then that sustainability education was my kind of activism. One of the songs from the Sea to Sky's "Sounds of Sustainability" repertoire sums up my journey of finding passion as a person and as an activist:

Go wild, let the wonder flow
Go wild, let the wisdom grow
And when you feel your heart go beyond your skin
And you know that's the way that it's always been
Tell me what are you waiting for?
Go wild, get yourself outdoors

There were no more reasons to wait before taking action. I'd logically reasoned and thought out my own definition of activism; now I *felt* it. A few years after that first visit to the island when I threw open the doors to activism, I'm feeling it more than ever.

I don't know yet if I want to teach in a school or work with popular education initiatives outside the classroom. However,

I do know that as an educator, I don't want to be confined by curriculum or school board mandates, I don't want to constrain students' energy and enthusiasm within four walls and credit requirements, and I don't want anything to do with existing conventions—I want to replace convention with community, care, courage, and consciousness. I want to inspire passion and encourage action. I want to be an educator for activism.

When I say the word "activist," don't think about the smoke bomb and bandana, forget the chains and the bulldozers, and tune out the angry chanting. When I say the word "activist," think of the possibilities, think of your passion, and think of yourself.

■ ■ ■ ■ ■

NATALIE GERUM is from Dundas, Ontario. She is a graduate of the Lester B. Pearson United World College and is currently studying at Mount Allison University as a Canadian Merit scholar. Natalie has served as a facilitator and program assistant for the Pearson Semi-

nar on Youth Leadership (www.psyl.ca), Sea to Sky Outdoor School (www.seatosky. bc.ca), and the CIStA Leadership Conference (www.cista.org). She is a coordinator for Eco-Action, a sustainability education program, and the Sustainable Residence Initiative, both at Mount Allison University.

Yuill Herbert

WHEN I USE the word "radical" I have its deepest, original meaning in mind. The *Oxford English Dictionary* defines the word as "Going to the root or origin; touching or acting upon what is essential and fundamental; thorough." I've been lucky in my life so far to have belonged to some strong, radical communities, with rooted connections to people and place. These communities have given me the space and encouragement to be involved in unusual projects—like helping to found the Tatamagouche Community Land Trust in the fall of 2003, a project inspired by my childhood connection to the land.

My first roots are in Salmon Arm, British Columbia, where I grew up in a rural area without a television. I missed out on the cartoons, and in high school I didn't follow the soaps. In many conversations at school I was left out and I felt "different."

But not having a TV in my life gave me time, and I used that time to discover the forest.

The forest begins about fifty steps from the basement door at my parents' place near Gardom Lake, and it goes on for a long way. Towering over the forest is a cliff, a magical place. The forest around my house is a tangled mix of cedar, fir, spruce, white pine, and birch, but the top of the cliff is a meadow guarded only by widely spaced ponderosa pines that seem to gaze curiously out into the valley. I've often followed their example. From the cliff it's possible to see everything that happens below: farm tractors turtling around fields in endless circles, noisy little cars rushing to and fro, cattle meditating on the grass, and canoes lazing on Gardom Lake.

I came to know the other creatures that visited the cliff, like the ravens and red-tailed hawks that flew beneath the ponderosas and me. For two years in a row a family of great horned owls lived in the pines. Every time I climbed up there they would alight from their perch to my delight. I also found out that before I was born, cougars used to live in a cave on the face of the cliff. A farmer believed they threatened his winter bacon—the deer population—and shot them. After I learned about the cougars I could feel their absence, a missing wildness.

When you get to know a place intimately and something threatens it, that something threatens you, too. I felt such a threat when a neighbouring family decided to log their land. Logging seemed brutal and harsh, and I couldn't understand their motivation. My brother and I decided on a course of radical action. Inspired by the environmental writer Edward Abbey—whom I'd discovered at the local library—and a hearty dose of teenage righteousness, we placed spikes in the path of the logging machinery. We got caught, and the resulting multi-year conflict with our neighbour gave us serious doubts about what we had done. But, as the forest became a slash pile, my regrets about my actions didn't dampen my sense of loss.

Once your eyes are opened to injustice, it's hard to close them again. In my explorations of the forest I'd found several veteran old-growth trees that dwarfed their neighbours. From my vantage point on the cliff I used to imagine how the now agricultural valley below used to look when it was filled with such majestic trees. Prompted by my discovery of these trees and the experience with my neighbours, I began to study the ecological impacts of clear-cutting. I joined a local environmental group that worked to preserve two pristine valleys north of Shuswap Lake and to prevent clear-cutting in the region by organizing hiking trips and public debates and by writing letters.

Then in the summer of 1992 I followed the protests at Clayoquot Sound carefully, since I was too young to make the journey there myself. Every day I cut out newspaper articles that covered the protests; I still have that file of yellowing clippings. Over one thousand people were arrested in the non-violent protests against the clear-cutting of ancient temperate rain forest—one thousand people who felt so deeply connected to Clayoquot Sound that they spent up to four months in jail.

As I grew up my interest in ecological and social issues grew wider, at least in a geographical sense. I joined protests around North America against an alphabet soup of organizations: the WTO (World Trade Organization), the WPC (World Petroleum Congress), the G8 (Group of Eight), the FTAA (Free Trade Agreement of the Americas), and the SOA (School of Americas). I was pepper-sprayed and tear-gassed, an activist's form of penance. It was thrilling and inspiring to flood the streets with thousands of people in the name of social justice. But going to protest after protest was not leading to systemic change—and the constant cycle of reacting to threat after threat made me feel empty and cynical. The supportive culture of committed activists tempered this feeling—it was exhilarating to see a diverse group coming together with a common purpose—but there is a nugget of truth when the likes of *The Economist* glibly dismisses activists as "protest junkies."

So I upped my level of commitment and decided to try to tackle one of the biggest, most intimidating challenges that we face: climate change. In the summer of 2001 I cycled across Canada in the Climate Change Caravan, an initiative of a group of students at Mount Allison University. To me, the issue of climate change proved that social justice and ecological issues are inseparable: a small number of rich people, mostly in the rich countries, are guzzling fossil fuels at a grossly disproportionate rate and in so doing are causing hurricanes, floods, wildfires, and droughts that are literally killing poor people around the world. Those who are causing the least damage to the climate are suffering the most. For example, Andean farmers are losing their traditional crops due to drastically altered weather patterns, and they don't have the money to import food or seed. Our group wanted Canadians to understand that the ecological impacts of climate change have serious social implications.

The Climate Change Caravan included, at its peak, forty cyclists and a bus that ran on used vegetable oil (we filtered out french fries with old pantyhose) and featured a serious speaker system powered by solar panels and a wind turbine. We challenged the Canadian government to a bet that individuals could do more to reduce greenhouse gas emissions than government initiatives, and we aimed to win that bet. We gave hundreds of presentations in schools, town halls, churches, living rooms, and university lecture theatres. Our presentations informed people about climate change and then asked them to commit to an eight-point plan to reduce their personal emissions. The plan included simple and practical steps such as biking to work one day a week, turning down the household hot-water temperature, and using a clothesline. In Toronto, we shut down an Exxon gas station to protest the company's denial of climate change. In every city and some small towns across Canada, we held critical mass bike rides that took over the streets from cars. We held a funeral for the future—complete with a coffin and a priest—on Parliament Hill in Ottawa. We illegally cycled across the Confederation Bridge to Prince Edward Island to highlight the fact that it was the first major engineering project built for rising sea levels. Using a specially designed line-painting bike attachment, we outfitted Halifax with bike lanes.

Along our journey we would move into and out of church halls, school gymnasiums, and campgrounds, and we experienced the exhilarations and struggles of a type of communal living that is seldom found in a society based on the nuclear family—imagine a summer camp with a serious purpose and equally serious responsibilities. The strength of the group persevered in times when an individual would certainly have faltered: in four and a half months on the road we didn't miss a single day of our schedule despite extraordinary hurdles that ranged from a broken bus axle to flat tires, from rain storms to pure exhaustion. Our campaign went beyond simple reaction by promoting the benefits of what the Caravan itself embodied: long-lasting personal change supported by a strong community.

As our perhaps unrealistic hopes of mobilizing the entire Canadian population to tackle climate change evaporated—although people we encountered during our campaign had good intentions, we knew that breaking their dependency on cheap oil would require years of effort—the trip took on a new meaning. After almost five months on the bicycle seat and on the campaign trail, we came to an unexpected realization. On the Caravan we made changes thanks to our collective effort that would have been difficult for an individual to achieve: buying local organic food had become second nature for us, for example, and it was affordable when purchased in bulk. Our group's diverse interests and skills meant that each person found a niche, whether it was writing press releases or rebuilding bicycle hubs. And we built a culture around the bicycle as the primary means of transport. We came to believe that, as a collective, we would have more success implementing the radical personal lifestyle changes needed to help halt climate change.

When the Caravan ended in Halifax in October we scratched our heads for a long time trying to map out a next step. Someone in the group suggested we create a community land trust (CLT). Robert Swann, the founder of E.F. Schumacher Society, invented CLTs in Massachusetts in 1980. Like a corporation or a co-operative, a CLT is a legal structure that can be incorporated. But CLTs are radical in their premise that land, as much as air or water, is part of the common wealth and therefore shouldn't be owned or sold for profit. At the same time, the CLT protects the individual need for a secure place to live by providing the long-term right for individuals to use the land, and it assigns a fair value to any improvements that individuals might make. It is a system that balances the needs of both the community and the individual.

In the fall of 2003, after two years of scraping together money and looking for land, a group of Caravaners purchased a farm in Nova Scotia with the eventual aim of donating the land to the Tatamagouche Community Land Trust. The eighty-five acres had previously been a dairy farm in the hands of one family for almost two hundred years, and the father of the last owner, now in his seventies, still lives on a small piece of the land.

In the summer of 2005 we grew a hearty crop of vegetables and a weedy crop of heritage varieties of oat, barley, and wheat. We threshed the grain using a pre-1940s thresher, which resembles a Dr. Seuss machine, with belts and wheels everywhere. We built everything from a compost toilet to a greenhouse. We held amazing feasts and washed many dirty dishes. We raised chickens and ducks. We organized the annual Tatamagouche Summer Free School. At this school, anyone can teach anything, as long as he or she is passionate about the subject. In one day I learned about blacksmithing, the beauty of Euclid's proofs, and the history of residential schools.

I believe that in the Tatamagouche Community Land Trust we've found a community that includes both people and place. However, there are many questions we still need to address: How do we bridge the ideological and age gaps between the land trust and the wider community? How can we carry the model of the land trust beyond Tatamagouche? How do we ensure that it's both relevant and realistic for people of different classes and different beliefs? And how do we make the farm economically self-sustaining?

The answer to at least some of these questions lies in the land. When we were harrowing a field, local farmers stopped by to offer advice, and when we threshed the grain, people stopped just to watch, commenting that they hadn't seen a machine like the thresher run since the days of their grandparents. The land offers the opportunity to grow food to sell. So it is rooted. So it is radical.

If you happen to be in the neighbourhood, stop by. You will be welcome.

■ ■ ■ ■ ■

YUILL HERBERT is originally from Salmon Arm, British Columbia. In the summers he grows grains at the Tatamagouche Community Land Trust in Nova Scotia. In the winters Yuill works with Sustainability Solutions Group (www.sustainabilitysolutions.ca), a worker's cooperative, on sustainability assessments of organizations and green-building consulting. Yuill is also the environment editor of the *Dominion* newspaper (www.dominionpaper.ca).

Tim Harvey

IN SEPTEMBER 2004 cold Greenland air spilled across the Arctic to Chukotka. A dusting of snow on the lichen of mountain passes showed the footprints of wolverines, wolves, and bears. Next, October froze the tundra berries that carpet valley basins. In early November, as I limped near the end of a six-hundred-kilometre hike east of the Bering Strait with a young Russian woman and an ailing Canadian man, temperatures free-fell—wind seared our skin, and tears locked our eyelids shut.

We were in a bad way. My feet stung in torn leather boots so stiff I had to pull them on with pliers. The other Canadian, Colin Angus, would wake up literally frosty from the heavy sweating caused by a then-undiagnosed kidney infection. Yulia Kudryavtseva's leg had a palm-sized blister from a brittle fold in her rubber boot.

For me, the hardest moment came as I was walking through a wide, chest-deep river whose strong currents had kept it from freezing though the water's temperature was below zero. I knew as my feet and legs grew numb that if I fell, the river would wash me away. At such times the Arctic cold bit deep, as if to snuff out our inner flames of hope. But somewhere inside my aching, icicled, frost-nipped head, two convictions remained stronger than my urge to call in a rescue and get the hell out of there.

The first was my belief that if we all kept walking we could stay alive: movement alone would keep us unfrozen. The second idea related to my mission. The sting of Chukotka's cold underscored a truth found in Leo Tolstoy's memoirs: "If you don't regard your life as a mission, there is no life, only hell." I was convinced that by trekking through the bitterest chill north of Antarctica, we could stoke the fire of a global movement to preserve earth's most essential component: cold.

Cold, to minus sixty degrees Celsius and beyond, still occurs in Chukotka, the northeastern extremity of Asia. It's a wind-rippled land of grizzly and polar bears, ptarmigan, lemmings, birds, and Arctic hares. The abundance of life survives not despite the cold, but because of it.

Consider polar bears, which reproduce in the world's highest concentration of dens on Wrangell Island, a short walk from the floating sea ice on which they hunt. Algae growing under the ice support a food chain including plankton and fish, seals and walrus, polar bears and seabirds, which migrate from across hemispheres to nest in Chukotka. The 2004 *Arctic Climate Impact Assessment*, the work of over 250 scientists, predicts the seasonal loss of all sea ice within one hundred years—and with it, the extinction of polar bears. If the bears go, they won't be alone. A whole Arctic food chain will crumble beneath them.

In the windy, treeless wilds of Chukotka, over ten thousand indigenous people, the Chukchi, depend directly on the productivity of their frozen lands. Coastal Chukchi patrol the sea ice for walrus with hinged harpoon tips designed millennia ago. Their inland cousins camp on the tundra in home-sewn furs through winter's darkest months, raising families, building sleds of willow wood, and tending herds of reindeer as they have since times unknown. They live as nomads on the Arctic ice.

Hiking onto a plateau with a broad valley view, we found stone circles that served as foundations for *yarangas*, double-walled family domes of reindeer hide. Elsewhere, a cluster of old, grey antlers on a bed of piled stones marked where a sha-man once ushered a spirit to another world.

The Soviet Union nearly destroyed the Chukchi. In 1956 low-flying aircraft hunted the last free nomad. Herding became an industry with fewer, larger herds, and the walrus hunt was similarly intensified. Populations were concentrated in concrete towns like nuclear-powered Bilibino, where today, buildings are crumbling as the once-frozen soil thaws beneath them for the first time in sixty thousand years. When communism fell in 1991 Moscow cut regional subsidies to the Chukchi, leaving them to starve or relearn old arts of survival. Hunger and vodka claimed much of the population. The situation remains grave.

Yet Chukchi life might have stabilized if the effects of cli-mate change were not undermining Chukotka's ecosystems. Adapting their communities to changes in nature created by the accelerating climate trend is becoming the greatest chal-lenge the Chukchi have ever faced. To learn about and publi-cize their struggle is a major reason we plotted a route through the Chukchi's Arctic homeland.

Our tundra hike was only one stage of a more ambitious journey. From Vancouver to Moscow we were trying to propel ourselves over land, river, sea, and ice, without burning a drop of fossil fuel. If our journey to Moscow succeeded I would then challenge myself to return home without emissions. Our efforts would allow us to promote human power as a source of emission-free fuel that is a key to stabilizing our climate. Though cheap, fun, and accessible, human power remains for many people a paradigm shift away.

The idea that climate change is unstoppable, like a runaway train screaming down the Fraser Canyon, breeds apathy and defeatism. It's also simply untrue. We need to cut about 60 per cent from today's global carbon dioxide (CO_2) emissions for the climate to stabilize. Accomplishing this objective will take teamwork: a network of individuals doing whatever possible to minimize their own greenhouse emissions, united by the common goal of putting an end to human-induced climate change. The team will grow in lockstep with a rising awareness that whether we live in a modern metropolis or the remote Chukotka ice, we're all in this fight together. It's a matter of survival.

What you might grimly call the "survival paradigm," ironically, is all about celebrating life and having fun. It embraces the mindsets of challenge and adventure, which lead to problem-solving, self-fulfillment, and improved health. Applied to transportation, it rules out spending copiously on cars and fuel. It sends you whizzing past traffic jams and arriving energized and smiling to work or school—cyclists already keep thousands of tonnes of CO_2 out of the atmosphere. As the movement spreads, transmitted by smiles, our gains will multiply exponentially.

With this outlook in mind Colin and I cycled out of Vancouver in June 2004, bound for the Yukon River, the Bering

Sea, and then Chukotka, where Yulia would join us in September. We built an audience by radio, print, and television interviews from remote locations. We called for self-propelled living, a fun and healthy way to combat climate change.

I am a die-hard optimist, but realism told me the fight against climate change could use a few good mind bombs—a term coined by Greenpeace in the 1970s. Back then the group provided TV networks with footage of an industrial Russian harpoon shot like a cannonball just above an inflatable protest boat, then ripping into the backside of a whale. That one dramatic newsreel ended complacency about industrial whaling. Our challenge was to shatter complacency towards car culture, to shake the foundations of an ideology that values convenience first. I hoped to find the mind bombs we needed on the northern frontlines of climate change.

Cycling north from Vancouver, we soon spotted stands of reddish pine trees killed by beetles. Mountain pine beetles are exploding because winters are no longer cold enough to control their population. The beetles are poised to eliminate a dominant tree species from the ecology of the B.C. interior. Among other problems, all those dead, dry trees are ideal fuel for fire.

The B.C.-Yukon border region felt like a war zone. Flames curled on hillsides like burning oil wells, embers flashed in the wind, and helicopters dropped tanks of lake water over mushrooming columns of smoke. Anticipating the worst, Swift River locals soaked their wooden houses and café with hoses as hundreds of trucks and RVs, and two laden cyclists pulled over where the highway was officially closed. We loaded our bikes into a canoe on the upper Yukon River and paddled into a haze in which trees glowed and moose swam through a gentle shower of ashes.

The fire season was setting records in the Yukon, the new norm in the era of climate change. Hurricane seasons are likewise growing longer and more intense each year as ocean temperatures rise in the Caribbean. The flames engulfing us were part of a global trend: melting glaciers, continental droughts, and flooded cities. If today is bad, then the future of climate change defies our capacity to imagine.

WE COULD SEE smoke trickling up from a *yaranga* in a snowy Chukotka valley. Reindeer were digging for lichen as a fur-clad father and son kept a vigil for wolves. What they saw that February afternoon were three backcountry skiers approaching— our team: Colin had just returned from urethral surgery; Yulia and I had passed winter's darkest months in Anadyr, Chukotka's capital, plotting the way forward along frozen rivers and abandoned road beds in boreal East Siberia. Finally back on the ice all together, we saw the two Chukchi raise their reindeer mittens and invite us over to warm up with roast meat and tea.

Approaching the *yaranga* as three generations of family emerged to greet us with beaming smiles—this meeting was the sort of scene I envisioned when the expedition was still a dream. At such times I often wished an old friend, Jonathan Hungerford, were there to share the adventure.

All too briefly, Jono and I shared a house near the University of Victoria, where we were students. Relative to the *yaranga*, the old farmhouse was a monument to extravagant living. One of our bonds was that Jono and I had both witnessed widespread poverty in Latin America and realized just how good we had it. Jono also realized how good it was simply to be alive, having beaten lymphatic cancer during his final year of high school.

In his first term of university, Jono read *One River* by Canadian ethnobotanist Wade Davis and promptly hatched plans to travel in South America. Jono was inspired by Davis's research in Andean and Amazonian cultures, where the writer soaked up knowledge both scientific and spiritual. Davis then shared the wonder of rare cultures with an impassioned call to preserve human and natural diversity. Jono felt a similar calling.

Exploring Peru, Ecuador, Colombia, and Brazil, Jono floated the Amazon, rehabilitated an orphaned jaguar, received the healing of a rainforest shaman, and slept amid pre-Colombian ruins. He sensed a soft-spoken power and wisdom in these people and places and a reverence for nature not found in mainstream Western culture. Spared by cancer, and inspired by South America and the writings of a cultural botanist, Jono decided to complete a degree in biology and then further explore the earth while working with others to tread lightly upon it. A natural leader and self-deflating humorist, Jono had the daring and confidence to realize any dream. The first time he tried on telemark skis he landed a back flip, because he believed he could.

Cancer gave Jono a commitment to health. He sold his old Bronco, bought a bike, and built his physique into an impressive exemplar of strength and agility honed on the soccer field, in a kayak, on mountain hikes, and through kick-boxing. Then tragically, still shy of his twenty-second birthday, cancer dealt Jono a second, more serious blow.

Before he died in Vancouver, Jono visited Victoria for a potluck with his university friends. He was bald from chemotherapy but still a beacon of uplifting energy. The theme of the evening was how to create social change, and Jono proposed an informal group called "Small Feet" to signify the reduced environmental footprint we would promote through education and example. The group wasn't about making a legacy for Jono or the people in that room—it was about the legacy of our generation. Would we leave the earth toasting in a blanket of greenhouse gases, or could we create a place of bicycle-friendly cities, urban agriculture, and fulfilling lives with little impact on nature?

The young people at the potluck had various interests and origins, but all were enthusiastic to make their lives a model of the healthy lifestyles required to heal our planet. They were an embodiment of our generation's values and resilient optimism. More than any generation before us, ours has the vision and spirit, the tools and the passion to achieve our dream of a liveable earth. For many of us losing Jono was a call to harness our dreams.

Mine carried me, eventually, through the fur curtain door of a *yaranga*, over a threshold between worlds. We stepped out of the harsh beauty of the Arctic, a valley so still, we could hear the reindeer chew. Inside the *yaranga* was a capsule of warmth holding the smells, language, and artifacts—the spirit—of a people who live on the edge of the world. Shadows obscuring its edges made the dome feel infinite. We settled on fur mats alongside kids in one-piece pyjamas still sporting dogs' ears on the hood, as an elder named Taya stirred bowls of tea. Meat sizzling on a *yaranga*'s central fire and the sounds of spoken Chukchi were a scene hardly changed in centuries.

But the basics of life were changing faster than the Chukchi could anticipate. On the northern coast one in five whales brought ashore, in recent years, has been classified a "smelly whale," so highly toxic the dogs won't eat it. Walrus are washing up dead for reasons unknown. According to Taya's family, the reindeer herders of Chukotka's interior are facing similar difficulties.

Speaking to us in Russian, the Chukchi explained the difficulty of rebuilding herds almost entirely consumed during the hungry years after communism was overthrown. I expected to hear about tundra fires or exotic reindeer diseases, but the

issue on their mind was wolves. Probably due to the myste-
rious, steady decline of Arctic hare, Chukotka's wolves are
depending more heavily on reindeer. They stalk a herd during the long winter nights, only backing off when millions of
rodents emerge in the spring. The spring melt, however, only
compounds the troubles of the Chukchi.

Today Chukotka's snow melts at least a month earlier than
elders like Taya remember, transforming a world of ice into
a world of watery mud, since liquids can't drain through soil
still frozen half a metre underground. Predictably, the season
of sled runners sliding freely over snow grinds to a muddy halt,
crippling the ability of Chukotka's nomads to move.

Bright spring days are traditionally the highlight of the
Chukchi world, a reward for enduring the blizzards and darkness of winter. Spring days are longer, but the ground should
remain firmly frozen. It is the season of easy travel and festi-
vals when families meet, dance, and make music, wrestle and
race reindeer. But as spring grows ever shorter, it becomes a
time to drive herds north as quickly as possible, to reach the
mosquito-relief zones near the windy Arctic coast before being
trapped in the mud bogs. Losing the race against the end of the
frozen season can mean leaving the sleds behind and forging
on by foot, slow and wet, over rising rivers and across moist,
spongy valleys. For the clouds of mosquitoes and bot flies that
emerge in this season, humans and reindeer present a perfect
slow-moving meal. It is little wonder that as climate change
progresses, so many Chukchi youth are opting for life in Russian towns, where unemployment and alcoholism among the
indigenous are a continuing crisis. I realized then that the
youngsters in that *yaranga* might be forced off the tundra
before they grow old if the climate continues to warm.

I was never able to collect a graphic, TV-format mind bomb
like Greenpeace managed to do with Russian whaling. I didn't

have footage of a Chukchi family mired in mud as the tundra burned and flaming oil wells darkened the sky. But maybe such footage would isolate the issue, like an oil spill that needs mopping up. The Greenpeace whaling action sent shockwaves through society, but it didn't foster a deep understanding of nature's infinite connectivity or the essential oneness of humans, nature, and the earth itself. Today's environmentalism looks beyond single issues, because every one of them, like the story of the Chukchi, is a window into a common problem. Consumer lifestyles are driving the snow out from under the sleds of the Chukchi. We still don't have small feet.

The best and fastest way to shrink our shoe size is to park our cars—at a recycling facility, ideally—and jump on a bike. Our own health and longevity are reason enough, but given the global consensus on the implications of climate change, we also owe it to vanishing cultures like the Chukchi, and future generations worldwide, to heal this ailing planet one pedal at a time.

■ ■ ■ ■ ■

TIM HARVEY was brought up in a canoe and has worked as a wilderness guide and kayak instructor. In 2003 his photographs of endangered wilderness in Central America were featured in a cross-Canada

tour as part of the GAIA project, as well as in a national newspaper in El Salvador. In 2004–05 he wrote a twenty-seven-part adventure column in the *Vancouver Sun* and *Edmonton Journal*. At the time of writing Tim was completing a zero-emissions round-the-world journey with the twin aims of promoting greener lifestyles and inspiring others to pursue their dreams.

His adventures are chronicled at www.vancouvertovancouver.com and in a book to be released in 2007.

Environmentalism and Sustainability

WEBSITES

Center for Ecoliteracy *http://www.ecoliteracy.org*

DeSmogBlog *http://desmogblog.com*

Environmental Youth Alliance *http://www.eya.ca*

Post Carbon Institute *http://www.postcarbon.org*

Responsible Shopper *http://www.responsibleshopper.org*

Slow Food *http://www.slowfood.com*

Treehugger *http://treehugger.com*

BOOKS

Alan Weisman, *Gaviotas: A Village to Reinvent the World.*
   White River Junction: Chelsea Green Publishing
   Company, 1998.

Bill McKibben, *The End of Nature.* New York: Random
   House, 1989.

Charles Wohlforth, *The Whale and the Supercomputer: On
   the Northern Front of Climate Change.* New York: Farrar,
   Straus, and Giroux, 2004.

Daniel Quinn, *Ishmael: An Adventure of the Mind and Spirit.*
New York: Bantam, 1995.

Marq de Villiers, *Water: The Fate of Our Most Precious Resource.*
Toronto: McClelland and Stewart, 2003.

Michael Pollan, *The Botany of Desire: A Plant's-Eye View of
the World.* New York: Random House, 2001.

Steve Van Matre, *Earth Education: A New Beginning.* Greenville:
Institute for Earth Education, 1990.

Tim Flannery, *The Future Eaters: An Ecological History of the
Australasian Lands and People.* New York: Grove/
Atlantic, 2002.

Wade Davis, *One River.* New York: Simon & Schuster, 1996.

Politics and Democracy

WEBSITES
Canadian Centre for Policy Alternatives
http://www.policyalternatives.ca

Democracy Now! *http://www.democracynow.org*

The Democracy Project *http://www.thedemocracyproject.ca*

Democratic Renewal *http://www.democraticrenewal.com*

Fair Vote Canada *http://www.fairvotecanada.org*

BOOKS
John Ibbitson, *The Polite Revolution: Perfecting the Canadian
Dream.* Toronto: McClelland and Stewart, 2005.

Jamie Brownlee, *Ruling Canada: Corporate Cohesion and
Democracy.* Black Point: Fernwood Publishing, 2005.

John Ralston Saul, Alain Dubuc, and George Erasmus, *A
Dialogue on Democracy in Canada.* Rudyard Griffiths,
ed. Toronto: Penguin Canada, 2002.

Michel Foucault, *The Foucault Reader.* New York: Pantheon
Books, 1984.

Paul Howe, *Strengthening Canadian Democracy*. Montreal: McGill-Queen's University Press, 2005.

Social Justice and Human Rights

WEBSITES

The Council of Canadians *http://www.canadians.org*

Derechos: Human Rights in Sub-Saharan Africa
http://www.derechos.org/human-rights/afr/#web

GapMinder *http://www.gapminder.org*

Margo Pfeiff, "Humanities 101." *Reader's Digest*
http://www.readersdigest.ca/mag/2003/08/humanities.html

Universal Declaration of Human Rights
http://www.un.org/Overview/rights.html

World On Fire *http://www.worldonfire.ca*

BOOKS

Amin Maalouf, *The Crusades through Arab Eyes*. New York: Schocken, 1989.

Earl Shorris, *Riches for the Poor: The Clemente Course in the Humanities*. New York: W.W. Norton, 2000.

Greg Paul, *God in the Alley: Being and Seeing Jesus in a Broken World*. Colorado Springs: Shaw Books, 2004.

Jack Layton, *Homelessness: The Making and Unmaking of a Crisis*. Toronto: Penguin, 2000.

Jeffrey D. Sachs, *The End of Poverty: Economic Possibilities for Our Time*. New York: Penguin, 2005.

John Stackhouse, *Out of Poverty: And Into Something More Comfortable*. Toronto: Random House Canada, 2000.

Joseph Heath and Andrew Potter, *The Rebel Sell: Why Culture Can't Be Jammed*. Toronto: HarperCollins Canada, 2004.

Race Relations and Decolonization

WEBSITES

Canadian Race Relations Foundation *http://www.crr.ca*

National Anti-Racism Council of Canada *http://www.narcc.ca*

BOOKS

Chinua Achebe, *Things Fall Apart.* Portsmouth:
Heinemann, 1971.

Edward W. Said, *Orientalism.* New York: Vintage, 1979.

Frantz Fanon, *The Wretched of the Earth.* New York: Grove/
Atlantic, 1986.

Nelson Mandela, *Long Walk to Freedom.* London: Back
Bay Books, 1995.

Patricia Hill Collins, *Black Feminist Thought: Knowledge,
Consciousness, and the Politics of Empowerment.* London:
Routledge, 1999.

Paulo Freire, *Pedagogy of the Oppressed.* London: Penguin, 1996.

Taiaiake Alfred, *Peace, Power, Righteousness: An Indigenous
Manifesto.* Don Mills: Oxford University Press
Canada, 1999.

Toni Morrison, *Beloved.* New York: Knopf, 1987.

International Development and Co-operation

WEBSITES

BBC World Service Trust *http://www.bbc.co.uk/worldservice/trust*

Canadian International Development Agency
http://www.acdi-cida.gc.ca/index.htm

BOOKS

Amin Maalouf, *In the Name of Identity: Violence and the Need to
Belong.* New York: Penguin, 2003.

Jennifer Welsh, *At Home in the World: Canada's Global Vision
for the 21st Century.* Toronto: HarperCollins Canada, 2004.

Michael Edwards, *Future Positive: International Co-operation in the 21st Century*. London: Earthscan Publications, 2001.

Ryszard Kapuscinski, *The Shadow of the Sun*. Toronto: Knopf Canada, 2001.

First Nations
WEBSITES

Ghost River Rediscovery
http://www.ghostriverrediscovery.com

Nunavut Arctic College, *Interviewing Inuit Elders*
http://www.nac.nu.ca/publication/index.html

BOOKS

Frank James Tester and Peter Kulchyski, *Tammarniit (Mistakes): Inuit Relocation in the Eastern Arctic 1939–1963*. Vancouver: UBC Press, 1994.

J. Edward Chamberlin, *If This Is Your Land, Where Are Your Stories?: Finding Common Ground*. Toronto: Knopf Canada, 2003.

Jack Hicks, *Nunavut: Inuit Regain Control of Their Lands and Their Lives*. Copenhagen: International Work Group for Indigenous Affairs, 2000.

John Bennett and Susan Rowley, *Uqalurait: An Oral History of Nunavut*. Montreal: McGill-Queen's University Press, 2004.

Marc G. Stevenson, *Inuit, Whalers and Cultural Persistence: Structure in Cumberland Sound and Central Inuit Social Organization*. Don Mills: Oxford University Press Canada, 1996.

Penny Petrone, *Northern Voices: Inuit Writing in English*. Toronto: University of Toronto Press, 1988.

Peter McFarlane, *Brotherhood to Nationhood: George Manuel and the Making of the Modern Indian Movement*. Toronto: Between the Lines, 1993.

Youth Leadership and Engagement
WEBSITES

Canada25 *http://www.canada25.com*

Magna's "Next Great Prime Minister" competition
*http://www.magna.com/magna/en/responsibility/community/
asprimeminister/default.aspx.*

Pearson Seminar on Youth Leadership *http://www.psyl.ca*

Youth Challenge International *http://www.yci.org*

The Centre of Excellence for Youth Engagement
http://www.tgmag.ca/centres

Global Youth Action Network *http://www.youthlink.org*

Taking it Global *http://www.takingitglobal.org*

Youth in Philanthropy Canada *http://www.yipcanada.org*

Youth.gc.ca *http://www.youth.gc.ca*

Youth Venture *http://youthventure.org*

Entrepreneurialism and Corporate Social Responsibility
BOOKS

Andrew Savitz and Karl Weber, *The Triple Bottom Line: How Today's Best-Run Companies Are Achieving Economic, Social and Environmental Success—and How You Can Too.* Mississauga: John Wiley and Sons Canada, 2006.

Dee Hock, *Birth of the Chaordic Age.* San Francisco: Berrett-Koehler, 1999.

Flora MacLeod, *Forming and Managing a Non-Profit Organization in Canada.* North Vancouver: Self-Counsel Press, 1995.

Mary Choquette and Peri Lynn Turnbull, *Emerging Practices in Corporate Social Responsibility Management.* Ottawa: Conference Board of Canada, 2002.

Michael A. Sand, *How to Manage an Effective Nonprofit Organization: From Writing and Managing Grants to Fundraising, Board Development, and Strategic Planning.* Franklin Lakes: Career Press, 2005.

Peter Drucker, *Managing the Non-Profit Organization: Principles and Practices.* New York: HarperCollins, 1992.

Spiritual Activism and Body Image

WEBSITES

About-Face *http://www.about-face.org*

Antidote: Making Change Possible
http://www.antidote.org.uk

ScaredSacred *http://www.scaredsacred.org*

■ ■ ■

THIS BOOK WOULD not be in your hands without the support and advice from many remarkable people. Severn Cullis-Suzuki, Kris Frederickson, Ahmed Kayssi, and Cynthia Mackenzie would like to thank Sam and Fran Belzberg and Jack Blaney, who partnered with the Department of Canadian Heritage to give the four of them the opportunity to embark on the wonderful journey of their Action Canada fellowship that culminated in this book. They are grateful to Cathy Beehan and the Action Canada team for their enthusiasm for this project, and especially to their mentor, Professor Mark Winston, who never hesitated to give support and share with them many invaluable insights. They would like to thank Greystone Books, for believing in this book, and their editors, Daniel Aldana Cohen, Iva Cheung, and Nancy Flight for their patience and wisdom in dealing with the havoc of twenty-five authors!

Thanks to the talents and interest of Shawn Woods for the evolutions of their website. Thank you to Chris Tabor of the Queen's University Campus Bookstore, who was generous with his advice. Finally their gratitude goes to all of the individuals who contributed essays to this volume. Thanks for your drive and dedication to what you do and for your patience and effort in this project. This book is here because of you.

Daniel Aldana Cohen would like to thank David Wachsmuth, who provided invaluable intellectual and emotional support. He would also like to thank Carmen Diana Dearden, who was the perfect host; her Caracas home and offices were lovely and essential to the completion of this book.

SEVERN CULLIS-SUZUKI has been using her voice since she was a kid. At the age of nine, she founded ECO, the Environmental Children's Organization. Three years later ECO attended the 1992 Earth Summit in Rio de Janeiro, where Severn delivered a powerful plenary speech that was later turned into her first book, *Tell the World*. She has continued to speak out all over the world, in the media, and at the UN, and she served on the Earth Charter Commission, Kofi Annan's Special Advisory Panel for the 2002 Johannesburg Summit. She is currently in grad school studying ethnobotany.

KRIS FREDERICKSON is a proud Métis engineer from Stonewall, Manitoba, who holds B.Sc. and M.Sc. degrees in biosystems engineering from the University of Manitoba where he researched water treatment options for Aboriginal communities. He has spoken frequently to Aboriginal youth about pursuing post-secondary education and in 2004 was recognized with a prestigious National Aboriginal Achievement Award. Currently Kris works as a water management engineer for Nexen, an international energy company, and co-chairs 2335, an initiative of the United Way of Calgary to increase youth engagement in the community.

AHMED KAYSSI holds dual bachelor's degrees in engineering chemistry and business German and an M.Sc. in physiology from Queen's University. He is currently enrolled in medical school. As a native Iraqi who lived in Egypt and Saudi Arabia before calling Montreal home, one of his passions is to raise awareness of the place newcomers have within Canada. At Queen's University, he founded the Arab Students Association and organized and moderated panel discussions on free speech and Canada–U.S. relations.

CYNTHIA MACKENZIE is a passionate human rights activist who is currently pursuing her doctorate in political science in Melbourne, Australia. She has worked on human rights projects around the world, from sex-worker outreach in Calgary and refugee advocacy in Vancouver to community development in India and Costa Rica and urban environmental projects in Cuba. She has been actively involved in Canada's public policy debate with Canada25. For her work, Volunteer Calgary named her a Leader of Tomorrow, and Maclean's has called her one of Canada's 100 Faces of the Future.

After growing up in Toronto, DANIEL ALDANA COHEN obtained a B.A. in the history of ideas and international development studies from McGill University in Montreal, where he was the editor of the independent student newspaper, The McGill Daily. He has raced the 800 metres at the Canadian Junior Championships, canoed into James Bay, and camped amid Inca ruins. He has lived and studied in Paris and the south of France and worked as a freelance journalist in Venezuela and Bolivia.